Praise for Plant...

Catherine Niggemeier represents the values we applaud most in the plant-based community. First off, she is a self-starter! Many of the influential needle-moving milestones in the plant-based diet movement have come through sheer initiative from private citizens using their own funding. More than twelve years ago, Dr. T. Colin Campbell decided he'd had enough pushback from governmental and health care interests. He decided to take his message to the people by laying out the key findings of the research he had done with taxpayer funding. With the help of his son Tom, he wrote *The China Study*. Despite the naysayers and initial publisher rejections, Dr. Campbell's book has already sold more than two million copies. Several translations later, it continues to make an impact on people all over the world.

I was fortunate to be asked to produce the film *Forks Over Knives* with private funding and saw first-hand what an impact this "home-made" message had on film and books. When Nelson and Kim Campbell were promoting our privately funded film *PlantPure Nation* on a publicity tour, their paths crossed with Catherine. All of us on the traveling crew were swept up in her enthusiasm,

and her food was amazing, too! These days we are swimming upstream against billions of dollars' worth of advertising, messaging, and lobbying from those people interested in preserving the status quo with the unhealthy standard American diet. Spreading the word about our healthy eating lifestyle can be daunting, but as the tagline for *PlantPure Nation* states, "The truth is a stubborn thing, it doesn't go away!"

We need to keep reporting on success stories to keep this amazing diet at the forefront of social media, in books, films, blogs, websites, etc. One by one, more and more people will catch on to the value of improved health and lifestyle through plant-based eating, and I am convinced they are more receptive when it comes without an agenda. Catherine does this already with her cooking classes and local outreach. Now she is sharing her advice—and these fantastic recipes—beyond Long Island so that more people can share in her happiness. Thank you, Catherine, for your support and your self-starting spirit—your enthusiasm is contagious!

— John Corry
Producer, *Forks Over Knives*

"Catherine is an extremely talented plant-based cook and educator. While screening *PlantPure Nation*, Catherine hosted the Campbell family for a lunch at her home, where she served us a smorgasbord of delicious dips, sandwiches, soups, and so much more. Her recipes incorporated whole foods with no added oils, which is so refreshing in the culinary world. Catherine truly has a gift for educating and motivating people into this lifestyle with easy and delicious plant-based recipes. I cannot wait to try more delicious recipes from Catherine such as her No Cheese Quesadillas, UnBeetable Burgers, Stromboli, and most of all the Mushroom Stroganoff."

— Kim Campbell
Author, *The PlantPure Nation Cookbook*

"In 2015, we took our new film, *PlantPure Nation*, on a national tour. I will always remember coming through Long Island and landing in Catherine's kitchen, spending an afternoon in good company and enjoying a delicious home-cooked meal. I especially enjoyed learning of Catherine's passion for the message of plant-based nutrition and the wonderful work she has done in her own community. Catherine is the perfect example of what it will take to change the world around this health message. Change will not be dictated from the top down by government and industry but will come through the inspired work of people like Catherine, someone I will always call a friend."

— Nelson Campbell
Executive Producer, *PlantPure Nation*

Plant to Plate

COOKBOOK

WITH CATHERINE NIGGEMEIER

Food photography and cover photo © 2017 Timothy Butler. Page 1, 2, 3, 4, 5, 6, 7, 11 (note paper), and single watermelons, grapefruits, oranges, kiwis, and limes © Shutterstock. Page 17 and 127 © Catherine Niggemeier

The author of this book does not dispense medical advice or prescribe the use of any technique as a form of treatment for physical, emotional, or medical problems without the advice of a physician, either directly or indirectly. The intent of the author is only to offer information of a general nature to help you on your quest for emotional and spiritual well-being. In the event you use any of the information in this book for yourself, the author and publisher assume no responsibility for your actions.

ISBN 13: 978-1-5333-4290-4
ISBN 10: 1533342903

Plant to Plate
EDUCATION
WITH CATHERINE NIGGEMEIER

www.planttoplateeducation.com

Plant to Plate logo design by Keith Frawley Illustration
Cover design and interior formatting by Tugboat Design

Love and Thanks

To my amazing husband, Steven,
who has been right by my side every step of the way.
None of this would have been possible without you,
and I am blessed to share my life with you.

To my beautiful girls, Hannah and Ava, you are everything to me,
and I am proud that God made me your mom.
I wish you a life filled with faith, fun, and good health, always!

To Mom,
your continuous prayers, love,
and support have always guided me,
and I am forever thankful.

To Dad,
the best supporter a girl could wish for.
Your love and pride is always there for me.
I know I am a lucky girl!

Contents

"Never think you are too old or too ill to make lasting, rewarding changes to your health!"
~ Catherine Niggemeier,
Plant to Plate

Foreword

The Plant to Plate Cookbook is a very likable book, both for the information it contains and for the personal and very sincere way it is presented. The evidence for this dietary lifestyle is now more than sufficient to say that the whole-food, plant-based diet is the most important development in human health care that has come along in decades. There is nothing like it, because not only does this dietary lifestyle prevent future health problems, but even much more significantly, it can be used to treat many already diagnosed diseases. Indeed, I am confident that it has more to offer than all the existing pills and procedures combined!

We all know that for many people, changing to this diet may be a challenge because of their being profoundly accustomed to their present diet—high in fat, sugar, salt, convenience foods, and animal-based foods. But we now also have evidence showing that a diet high in fat, sugar, and/or salt actually leads to real physiological addictions, and like any other addiction, it may take some time and a good dose of will power to get through. On the other side, however, new tastes emerge, and before long, we like food like never before—at least, that is what it did for me and our family, and it seems to be common knowledge.

Catherine addresses the commonly asked question concerning whether it is necessary to make a 100% transition to get its health benefits. She does it in a way that both empathizes with those who find the transition difficult, yet still encourages the idea that going the whole way is best. She does not want to cause a guilt complex if someone slips up from time to time, while still being supportive. This somewhat tricky terrain resonates with me because I cannot say that the science demands total conversion to get the health benefits. We know that some people can do all the wrong things, yet still have a long, reasonably healthful life. But at the same time, I also advocate 100% compliance because I don't see evidence that it is harmful, because a total switch enables taste preferences to change within a few months—or less—and because a total switch could be crucial for anyone experiencing an impending serious disease. In this way, I think that we can be accommodating yet also be true to the science.

This message is life changing, as this author can attest, and for those new to this idea, this book is a good place to start.

~ T. Colin Campbell, co-author of *The China Study*
Jacob Gould Schulman Professor Emeritus of
Nutritional Biochemistry, Cornell University

"With plants create your own sunshine on your plate!"
~ Catherine Niggemeier,
Plant to Plate

Author's Note

The information provided in *The Plant to Plate Cookbook* is not meant to replace professional medical advice.

The following is meant to inspire you to incorporate more plants into your diet, to nurture a love for eating plants, to show you the possible health benefits, and to give you inspiration for sharing whole-food, plant-based recipes with family and friends.

Speak to your health practitioners about whether eating a whole-food, plant-based diet is right for you.

I hope that readers will take my message of plant positivity and my desire to spread the wonderful feel-good warmth that comes from eating a diet that is healthy for the environment, is cruelty-free, and can make you glow from the inside out.

With love,
Catherine

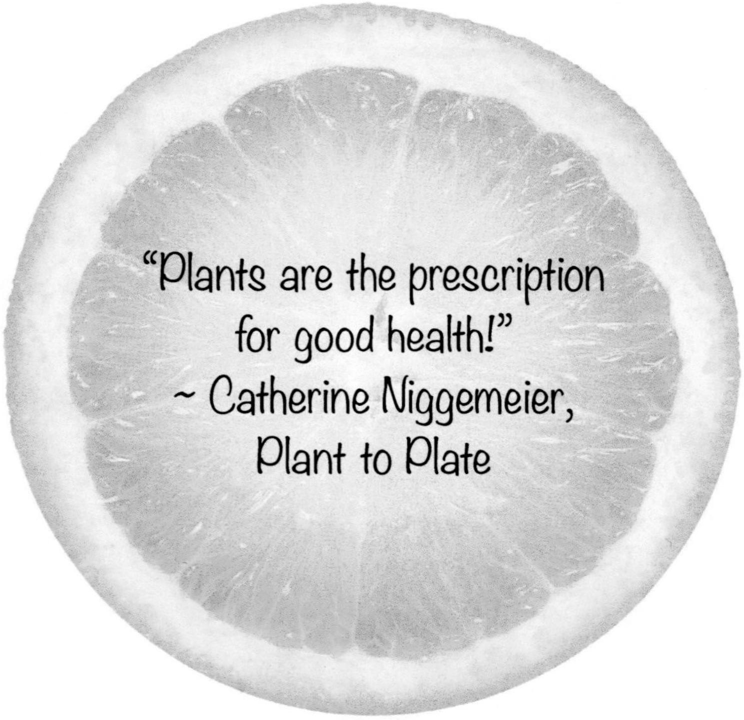

"Plants are the prescription
for good health!"
~ Catherine Niggemeier,
Plant to Plate

Introduction

How did you do it?

This is, without a doubt, the million-dollar question. When I meet someone I haven't seen in years, when people hear my story, when people see my energy level, this is the question that seems to be at the heart of it all. And that's understandable. After all, losing eighty pounds is no small feat. But losing those pounds isn't the most important part of my story; it almost never is for people who change their lives for the better by overcoming obesity. It's about keeping it off and living the best life possible. A life free of the constraints of dieting and the shackles of rigid measurements and diet products.

So how *did* I do it?

And this is where I just can't contain my enthusiasm: It's the plants! After a lifetime of riding on the frustrating roller coaster that is dieting, I'd finally found out what my body had been wanting all my life: plants.

When I tell people that I lost eighty pounds through whole-food, plant-based living, the look of anticipation at hearing the secret of my success turns to curiosity. I can see it written on their faces.

It's a common mental hurdle for people—the idea of giving up meat, dairy, and eggs—and it's really not their fault. Our society has trained us for so long to eat this way that the idea that our bodies may want something else can be almost impossible to accept. The idea that one has to go cold turkey (or maybe cold hummus? cold guacamole?) into giving up meat, dairy, and eggs can be too strong of a mental block for people, which is why I try to assure people that they don't need to drop all meat, dairy, and eggs from their diet tomorrow or next week or next month, but it should be something they strive for if they want optimum health and the success that I experienced. I did drop eating meat, dairy, and eggs immediately, and that's why I had the success that I did. Do what you need to do to eat more plants at every meal, and I'm confident that you'll eventually find the health benefits speaking to you through your body.'

> My philosophy is that any addition of plants to your diet is a good one. If you try one recipe and love it, then you've added more plants to your diet. And if you've added those plants to that one meal, then you might be open to adding another. That's the basis of the beauty of eating this way. Open your mind just a bit to let all those healthy plants in, and you'll find that your body responds in kind.

Mind Over Meat

I'd like to tell you a story. Years ago, in the early part of my journey into whole-food, plant-based living, my family was invited to a party. When heading to a party, I always bring something to contribute to the table. It's my way of thanking the host and sharing with others, and it also helps me to ensure that I have food I will enjoy.

Our gracious host was very welcoming, and he told me that I looked wonderful. But he also told me that he could never eat how I do because he's a man, and men need meat. I'd brought a tray of Hannah's Plant to Plate Hummus, along with a delicious bowl filled with quinoa, Israeli couscous, apples, walnuts, celery, and raisins—accompanied by a tray of roasted potatoes and peppers. I placed the dishes on the kitchen island of our hosts' beautiful home, and everyone started eating. Everyone loved my dishes, including Mr. Meat Eater. He said the food was great and that he loved it. His wife asked me for the recipe.

But at the end of the night, as the host saw us out at the end of the lovely evening in his home, me with my empty dishes in my arms, he asked me something curious. He wanted to know if I was okay. You see, he was concerned that I was still hungry because I didn't eat from the meat or cheese platters! That I hadn't had enough to eat. And I just thought it was so funny. He'd eaten my food, enjoyed it, watched all of his friends enjoy it, and yet was concerned that I wasn't satisfied. And the answer was of *course*! It really drove home to me how set we can be in our perception of nourishing ourselves—that we can be so convinced of foods we think our body needs, such as meat, dairy, and eggs, that the idea that we can live a full life without them can sometimes become difficult to see.

And the answer is: of *course* plants can satisfy you. Of *course* plants can nourish you. And best of all, your body will thank you for it. Add more plants to your diet, and you'll find that the enjoyment you get out of it can open your mind to otherwise unimaginable possibilities.

Remember: the plants are perfect so you don't have to be. Simply do your best to eat as much of them as you can.

Plant-Based Freedom

Along with the mental hurdle of thinking that one needs to eat meat, dairy, and eggs to have a happy body comes the misconception that eating plant-based means you will suddenly find yourself down that dreadful dieting gauntlet of negativity.

You must follow this diet plan exactly!

You must measure and account for every single thing you eat!

You can't eat that.

My philosophy of plant positivity chooses to focus not on what you can't eat, but on what you can. There are so many plants for us to eat, so

many ways for us to incorporate more plants into our meals. Eating plants doesn't mean only eating little bags of raw vegetables. With my Plant to Plate recipes, you can broaden your culinary horizons and find yourself eating delicious foods that leave you healthy and satisfied and energized.

I admit I spend a good amount of time shopping for plants for my family to eat. And I'm not ignoring the fact that we all lead busy lives. I lead a busy life as a wife to my husband, Steven, and as a mother to my two girls, Hannah and Ava. I run my business, Plant to Plate Education, teaching corporate wellness to employees and doing public speaking events.

The way I look at it is this: I know leading a healthy lifestyle requires some time and planning, but I would rather spend time shopping at the grocery store and cooking healthy meals than spending time sitting in the doctor's waiting room. Planning for health, living a whole-food, plant-based lifestyle, will make me less likely to spend time feeling tired and feeling sick in general. I encourage you, like me, to dedicate time to eating more plants; it's just a matter of realizing what we do with our time and how important our health is. I would rather spend my time with good health than spend my time dealing with declining health.

I first got this idea for changing my life for the better one day when Steve came home after taking his father to his monthly doctor's appointment. Steve is in law enforcement, and when he came home that day, he said something very innocently that struck a chord with me. He said that while he was waiting with his father, he realized something. He was seeing the same people in the waiting room every month—some of them quite young—and he felt bad about it. It reminded him of when young people get arrested and are in the criminal courts system. That once you're in the system, you're in the system, and it's very difficult to get out. But Steve is a positive guy and knows that if positive change happens, a person can get out of the system and thrive.

At the time, he wasn't speaking to me about

my lifestyle at all, but this one little comment from him had a profound impact on me. Was this where I was in life? Was I booked into the obesity system, destined to struggle to get out until the end of my days? How old would I be when I started sitting in the waiting room, waiting for prescriptions, diagnoses, or stern words from the doctor? I am thankful that I wasn't at that point, but my weight would have more than likely led me down this path.

Steve's passing words made me realize that I didn't ever want to be "arrested." I didn't want to be in any kind of system. The wheels began turning, and I knew that I had to do something different that would allow me the freedom of good health. And his words meant so much to me, even though I didn't mention it to him at the time. I was in relatively good health. I'd just been to my yearly doctor's checkup, and no one said anything to me about my weight. But I knew I was lucky that no diagnosis had been given, and I thought that if I didn't make changes now, that eventually that day would come.

I see people this way all the time now. I see it in social groups, in people I work with. I see it all around me. We're put into systems, and many times we have no idea how to get out without immense struggle. There are so many people who are breaking out of the system of type 2 diabetes, high blood pressure, high cholesterol, and reversing their heart disease through a whole-food, plant-based diet, and it is wonderful to be a part of their journey.

Eating plant-based is simpler than you've probably imagined, because you really can't mess up plant-based foods. If you like to cook in bulk, it's easy enough to do at the start of the week so that you can leave your fridge stocked with lots of food already prepared and ready to eat. At the very least, keep your fridge stocked with lots of plants that you can prepare easily. That way, when you are hungry, there's something for you to grab right away. Don't fear buying ready-made products at the store. People ask me all the time whether I soak my own beans, whether I bake my own bread, or make my own almond milk. And the answer is yes, I do, and I can. But I also don't balk at saving time by buying something from the store.

I have made hundreds of batches of almond milk, and so has my daughter, and one day we were at the market, and Hannah, who is the almond-milk maker of the family, saw a carton of Silk cashew milk. She wanted to try it, and the girls loved it, so that's what they drink now. We no longer make as much of our own almond milk, and that's completely fine with me. Just like any other family, we're busy, busy, busy, and for us, buying a ready-made product that still keeps us plant-based is worth the cost.

Yes, I can bake my own bread, but my family

also loves Ezekiel bread, so I buy that for us to eat. If I have time, I make the effort to soak my own beans just for fun, but we've all been in that not-so-fun situation when you are pressed for time and dinner has to be made *now* and you're stuck. So this is why I always have plenty of canned beans in the pantry ready to go. You can take a can of beans and rinse off as much of the sodium in it as you can and find yourself with a batch of beans already cooked and ready to be put into a plant-based recipe. Every day, we each eat at least a cup of beans, so you can imagine how many we have in our pantry! Have the foods that you need to make your busy life easy and manageable, and of course, whatever you can do to add more plants is an improvement to your day!

The Road to Plant to Plate Education

If you had told me years ago that I'd find myself running a business teaching people how to eat, that I'd make appearances on local television, appear in the newspaper, and become known as the healthy plant-based expert in my community... I would have laughed.

Like so many people with weight-loss stories out there, I was overweight for much of my life, and one of the biggest problems was my basic outlook as to *why* I was overweight. You see, I looked at my weight as a *fashion* issue, not a health issue. It was always about what I could look good in at my weight, whether a blouse made me look bad, or whether I could feel comfortable wearing certain clothes.

It took years before I came to realize that my dieting wasn't working because the way I was looking at weight loss was simply never going to work for me. Once I approached my weight loss from a true health perspective, once I realized the benefits of a whole-food, plant-based lifestyle, then the weight finally dropped off of me, and the focus on what I looked like wasn't as important. What became important to me was how I was feeding my body with food that would give me the best chance

to live a life free of the illness and medications that I may have ended up on due to my yo-yo dieting and weight.

In my twenties, I'd worked in the fashion industry—both as a spokesmodel and corporate trainer in sales and development for different companies in New York. For years, my weight had been kept in check by my career and the industry I was in. My appearance and my weight were a big a part of it, so I was able to keep my weight down, and getting paid to do that was certainly a perk.

But it's funny where life will lead you. Even though I'd enjoyed my career, I knew deep down that I wanted to have a career that would help people. I wanted to make a difference in people's lives.

I went back to school, and I received my Bachelor of Science degree in Community and Human Services in 2010. My parents, my siblings, my niece and nephew, Steve, and my girls were there at my graduation, and they were so proud of me. But the downside of this shining accomplishment of mine was the one that had been a problem for many years: my weight. At graduation that year, I was probably the heaviest I'd ever been.

As proud as we all were of me, I didn't do anything with my degree then. I was happy raising my daughters, watching with pride as they grew into healthy, athletic young girls. I must admit, at times I wondered if people wondered how my very athletic girls could have a mom who looked so unhealthy. I was so overweight. How could I be the mother to Hannah and Ava and yet have all this weight on me? I didn't realize then that the inflammation from eating lots of lean animal proteins was preventing me from shedding the weight I was trying so hard to get rid of.

Fashion had always been the driving force behind my need to lose weight. I never once thought about it from a health perspective. Today, that outlook is completely reversed, and health is at the forefront. Yes, I'm happy about what I can wear, but my health is always the priority.

I remember the final turning point, and funnily enough, it was fashion that came back to me once again. An invitation came in the mail, a beautiful wedding invitation. I walked to a mirror, invitation in hand, and I took a good, hard look at myself. A question rang through my mind: What am I going to wear?

And then it was as if everything came crashing down on me. I was so embarrassed. Was I going to diet yet again, only to gain it all back months later? Was I going to be the mother of the bride for Hannah and Ava one day while this overweight? I was tired. I was so tired of it all.

I had been looking into plant-based living. Celebrities left and right were losing weight and praising plant-based diets on talk shows, looking great on magazine covers after losing lots of weight. But it wasn't until I saw the film *Forks Over Knives* that something really clicked. I dove into the mindset that I'd eat only plants. Within a few days, I was feeling so great. I could not believe my energy and how great I was feeling. I knew with certainty that my weight was never going to define me again. I dropped everything I knew about diet and obsessing over my weight. I stopped letting my outside be the driving force behind my motivation rather than my inside, and I plowed ahead with my newfound plant positivity.

I've always been an early riser, but living plant-based suddenly sent my energy through the roof. So after a few days of Steve putting up with me waking up at 5:15 a.m. and talking a mile a minute, he finally asked me to wait until he woke up fully and could enjoy a conversation with me. But that just shows you how great I felt. I was sleeping better; I didn't feel tired. Every morning, I woke up energized and ready to take on the day. It was April 2014, and I felt fantastic.

The following month, I went to my niece's First Holy Communion, and one of her uncles came up to me and asked what was going on with me. He said I looked different. That I looked like I was *glowing*. And when

he said this, I just couldn't believe it. I had noticed the difference in my skin, in my energy, and as he was saying this to me, my mind was screaming at me: *It's the plants!* Of course, I didn't want to scare him, so I smiled and simply said thank you.

At that point, I think I'd lost thirteen to fourteen pounds. Remember, I've lost eighty pounds, so this was still fairly early in my plant-based journey, and that weight loss probably wasn't very noticeable, but what he *did* notice was my glow. That was such a light-bulb moment for me—that someone who didn't live with me, someone who didn't see me every day, noticed that glow, that plant-based glow. It really just affirmed for me that the plants were making all the difference. It's true so many people talk about the glow they get once they start eating a whole-food, plant-based diet, and it happened within a couple of weeks for me.

Within the first week of eating this way, I knew this was the answer I was searching for. I knew that my weight issue was going to go away. I felt so great that I told my sister, Geraldine, that I was going to lose so much weight and that I would no longer have to focus on weight loss—plants were going to do this for me. She is my best friend, and I know she wanted nothing more than for me to lose this weight, but I could see it in her eyes as she looked at me with a supportive but here-we-go-again look of sympathy. I'd tried so many times in the past, and my whole family was rooting for me, but they also knew how easy it was for me to bounce back into weight gain, and I could tell they figured I was going to go through the same diet cycle I'd been spinning around in before. Now that I've been living plant-based for more than three years, my sister knows that this is my passion and that I will always continue to live this way. She is still my best friend and couldn't be happier for my health and all that has come along with it.

That August, I found myself at the beach with other parents. One of my friends was telling me how great it was that I'd lost so much weight—approximately forty-five pounds in four months. She told me that I really should teach her how to cook this way, and I should teach people how to do it. I laughed it off in the moment, but I'm the type of person who, if someone asks me to do something, I feel compelled to do it. My background in sales training and development told me that I could probably teach people how to live this way, and my passion for plants, along with my results, made me think about doing so.

So I gave it more thought. And the more I thought about it, the more I realized that this was what I'd wanted years ago. I'd wanted to help people, and now here was someone asking me to help others. How could I say no?

The first step was certification. I was fortunate to come across the T. Colin Campbell Center for Nutrition Studies certification program at Cornell University, and I enrolled that winter. I studied and found that everything I was doing for my health felt more validated once I learned about the science of *The China Study*. It added more affirmation that what I was doing was the right thing. After obtaining my certification, I made plans to host my first Plant to Plate Education class with none other than the friend who planted the seed in my head that day at the beach. My first class had five people.

The week before the class, I was fortunate enough to attend a ceremony in New York City at the Cornell Club, where I would get to meet, in person, Dr. T. Colin Campbell, hear him speak, and share a delicious meal of plant-based foods. I've always thought it was a bit silly when people cried while meeting their idol or over meeting a celebrity, but I finally got a taste of that feeling for myself at the dinner. Dr. Campbell walked in the room and was standing in the same room as me. I asked Steve to take a photo of me with Dr. Campbell, my certificate in hand. I stood there talking to him, not quite keeping it together, telling him about how his science and his efforts had done so much for my own personal health. When it was over, I sat down across from Steve and just burst into tears. I would

have never have thought that I would receive my certification from his program and have the opportunity to talk with him and take a photo together. The experience was overwhelming, but in the best possible way.

To think that ten months ago I had sat on my couch, eighty pounds overweight, watching *Forks Over Knives* and listening to Dr. Campbell share his science. Then to actually meet him in person and thank him for all his hard work and dedication was just one of the best moments of my life. I think I blurted out to Steve that it was the best night of my life, and then I quickly corrected myself by saying, of course, after marrying him and having our two girls! What can I say? My emotions got the better of me. One of the best parts of this night was sharing it with Steve, my constant support.

At that dinner, they told us about their upcoming documentary *PlantPure Nation*. The morning after my night in New York City, I called Cornell University to offer to host a screening of the film in my hometown. They were polite but told me that it was being handled by the producers out in California, but they assured me that it would be out in the spring and there would soon be a schedule of showings around the country. I thought that was the end of it, and I simply made a mental note to go and see it once it was out.

A few days later, I hosted my first Plant to Plate Education class in my home with just five people. From there, things simply took off. I posted a photo on Facebook, and people saw the food and the fun and they started booking classes. Word spread. I got busier and busier—at one point I received ten requests for classes in one month. The response from people was amazing and overwhelming. My attendees loved the food. They loved what I had to say about plant positivity, and they loved hearing my own story.

In March 2015, Patty Corry, the wife of John Corry, the producer of *PlantPure Nation* and *Forks Over Knives*, called me from Los Angeles—yes, I got a call from Hollywood!—and wanted to know if I was willing to be an ambassador for the film

PlantPure Nation. Then Patty mentioned they needed a place to stop for lunch after screening the film in New York City and asked if I could suggest a place. Suddenly Patty asked me to host one of my cooking classes for Dr. Campbell; his son, Nelson Campbell, the executive producer and director of *PlantPure Nation*; and his wife, Kim Campbell, the cookbook author of *The PlantPure Nation Cookbook* and *The PlantPure Kitchen*, for a luncheon at my home. I couldn't believe my ears. I'm happy to report that I kept my cool, but inside, I was a jumble of emotions. I was ready to cry all over again because I was going to have Dr. Campbell in my own home, eating my food. I had thought that one of the most amazing moments of my life couldn't be topped after the dinner at the Cornell Club. I was overwhelmed. It secured in my mind that this was my path in life, and I knew that this was what I was going to be doing as my career.

When Patty called, Steve was upstairs sleeping after working an overnight tour. I told myself to give him more time to sleep, and then I'd give him my big news. This lasted all of thirty seconds, and I ran upstairs to tell him. I told him to please not panic, but that I had just been offered an amazing opportunity to host Dr. Campbell in our house for a Plant to Plate luncheon! He couldn't believe it; he was so thrilled for me. And so I began planning for his visit. It was such a busy time. I was teaching lots of classes and sharing my excitement for *PlantPure Nation*. Professionally, I couldn't have been happier!

In May, Dr. Campbell, with a film crew in tow, arrived at our home. They spent a beautiful afternoon with us, staying for four hours, eating my food and answering all of our questions. The *PlantPure Nation* show sold out, so I certainly fulfilled my role in being a good ambassador for the film. In the end, I received a signed copy of *The China Study*, and inside, Dr. Campbell had written, "Your food is as good as it gets." Wow! He loved the food and I loved the day!

Because of this success, I was invited onto a local news program. They came and filmed one of my cooking classes, and after that, things just exploded. More and more people were interested in better health and better eating, and I was so thankful for the support of Steve, who became my partner in the kitchen. It's all been such a blessing.

The Plant to Plate Cookbook

In the whirlwind that has been Plant to Plate Education, I have hosted more than a thousand people in cooking classes, and as fulfilling as that was, I reached a point where I could no longer continue offering cooking classes along with my corporate wellness programs and speaking engagements. That's where *The Plant to Plate Cookbook* comes in.

If you're still with me at this point, you've probably picked up on the fact that people love the food that I cook. There wouldn't be so much demand for my classes otherwise. In this book, you'll find more

than sixty of my favorite recipes for living plant-based and eating healthier.

The important thing to remember going into this cookbook and these recipes is that everyone's tastes differ. You don't need to follow everything exactly; adapting recipes into something that works for you and the people in your life is part of what I talked about earlier about the freedom of a whole-food, plant-based lifestyle. Think about how your family eats now. You don't have a different recipe for every day of the year, do you? No. You have a standard set of go-to recipes, and you build upon that to add variety to your menus.

Another thing to keep in mind is that you don't have to do this overnight. You don't have to force everyone in your family to join you. I often hear from people that they're reluctant to begin whole-food, plant-based living because their families wouldn't do it with them. It doesn't need to be that way. Be the person in your home to start it, and let them make their own choices. If they join you for a meal, great! If they don't, that's their choice as well. But the meals I make are so yummy and delicious that people end up loving the dishes despite what they may think going in.

Everyone's heard the old adage that the way to a man's heart is through his stomach. There's wisdom in that saying that can apply to everyone. I always say, if you can win people over with food, then you can win over your family, but until then, do your best to win yourself over. Start with you. Eat as many whole-food, plant-based meals as you can and build upon that. If you have a meal that is not plant-based, don't sweat it. Don't beat yourself up. Do not feel guilty. Simply make your next meal plant-based and move on.

Writing this book has made me look back at all the years I struggled, and I feel for the people going through that same lifelong uphill battle that I did. But you don't have to fight that battle all your life. You don't need to be in the system and spend hours of your life in the doctor's office or at the pharmacy. People are changing their lives for the better by going plant-based, and they are healthier, stronger, and happier for it.

If you can't go fully plant-based, that's okay. Simply do your best to eat as many plants at every meal every day, and you will have already added plant positivity to your life.

It took less than a year for me to lose eighty pounds. Let that sink in for a moment. It was like I was carrying my youngest, Ava, who is twelve, around with me all these years. Only this extra person who was weighing me down was not only potentially taking years off my life, but taking enjoyment *out* of my life. My weight was defining who I was and what I could do. It's a problem I no longer face.

Now you know my story. You know how I lost the weight. How I changed my mindset and am now doing what I've always felt I should be doing: helping others. And so now the question is no longer how I did it.

The question is: *Are you ready to eat more plants and improve your health?*

Here are some tips on how you can do it!

Happy & Healthy

When people hear me speak, I always tell them: Do what will make you happy and healthy.

As a reader of this cookbook, I don't want you to think that you must adopt an all-or-nothing attitude about whole-food, plant-based living *or else*. The complete dropping of meat, dairy, and eggs was something I was personally committed to, which led to my fantastic results. For me, it was easy. I took the mantra that if it is a plant, I will eat it, and if not, I won't. If you want to make a true change, then I suggest you go with my all-or-nothing approach. I ONLY ate plants. I did not waver. No matter where I was eating, it was and still is always plants. This may sound strict, but for me it isn't, because I value my health and enjoy the food I eat, and I benefit by feeling great!

Clients will often comment that it's so great that my entire family eats this way. Yes, it is true the meals I make here in my home are all plant-based and my family enjoys them, but it didn't start out that way. Although my enthusiasm for whole-food, plant-based living was obvious to them, I didn't tell them that they had to eat this way; it was just something that naturally occurred.

It basically goes back to the idea that if you feed people good, delicious food, they will eat it. I did not take a bullhorn and shout from the rooftops that we, as a family unit, are becoming plant-based. Instead I just served them the food and they liked it.

My two daughters, ages twelve and sixteen, love plant-based meals. They love to make their own plant-based dishes, and they certainly know as athletes how great the food makes them feel and perform. They are also typical young adults who go out with friends, and when they are in social situations, they eat the foods that some of their friends are eating. If I hear that they have had a slice of pizza in town, there's no need for me to worry. I promise, I let them back in the house without consequence. The best part is hearing them say how happy they are to have a plate of plants once they come back home!

I have heard clients say they tried it and it didn't last because their spouse or family wouldn't eat this way. That's okay. Let them make their own choice, and go back to why you want to do this for yourself. Children become what they know. It may not happen when you want it to, but by being a good example, it will have a positive influence on them, and they will remember you taking charge of your health and treating yourself well.

We are all responsible for ourselves. No one can make me eat any differently than I do today, so my advice is: Don't let other people's choices change your direction toward good health. There is enough seriousness in the world. Plant-based living should be fun. It should be easy, not tedious. Just do your best to eat more plants!

Just live it. Don't preach it. Make yourself an easy guest in someone's home. Bring something you enjoy and share it. Just as I can be put off by someone telling me that I shouldn't live this way,

others can be put off by telling them what they shouldn't eat. Be an example of good health and have others follow what you are doing. Don't be too rigid in your thinking—just relax and let lots of plants into your life.

This is what has worked in my home and with my friends and family. I love nothing more than when my mom or my sister tell me about a dish they made all from plants. My enthusiasm for plants is just that—enthusiasm. I am enthusiastic about plants and their benefits, but I never want to force my views on others. I would rather inspire and have people decide to try it on their own. If they have questions, I am more than happy to share my message of plant positivity.

Here are a few tips for a happy and healthy approach to bringing more plants into your life and onto your plate.

- Approach it with ease, because it *will* become easier.
- Take a positive approach to learning new recipes.
- Relish in your successes in the kitchen and quickly move on if it doesn't come out the way you had planned. Don't think because you made an error in something you cooked that plant-based living isn't for you. If we all stopped at our first mistakes, life would be boring and no fun!
- Take it slow. Think of the way you are currently cooking. Do you have 365 different dinner recipes? Probably not, so don't feel as though you must have a wide variety of different meals each night. Find your favorites and rotate them through. Just think: in your hands, you have more than sixty whole-food, plant-based recipes to try. You already have more than I started with!
- Investigate alternatives to foods that you currently eat. Think about the foods that you currently eat. Are they real foods or are they "food-like products?" If you are trying to find a plant-based food to replace your favorite sweet, find a plant that can give you the sweetness you are looking for. Fruits are amazing, filled with fiber and sweetness; they can be your go-to dessert
- Be kind to yourself. Don't get discouraged if you have a health condition that you want to change. For me, I am actually thankful for the weight I struggled with for so many years, because it makes me so much more appreciative of the great health I have now.

- Take pride in knowing you eat completely cruelty free. I know most people are either a dog lover or a cat lover, and I've noticed people even put themselves on teams: Team Dog or Team Cat. Why not add a few others to your team? Join Team Cow, Team Chicken, Team Fish, or Team Pig. Add one more member to your team and keep going. It's a great feeling knowing that I am helping animals and our environment.
- Find the beauty in everything you eat. Who doesn't like beauty around them? We can stand in awe of beauty at the ocean, at a beautiful sunrise or sunset. Think the same way about your food. Find the beauty in the plate you eat from. Create a plate of happiness in the colors of the food rainbow. Each plate I make brings happiness to me, and I am always thankful for the meal I am eating. I am thankful for how the food makes me feel, thankful for the benefits I know it is giving my body, and thankful that I am on a path of good health each day.

I'm often asked, "Catherine, how can you be happy knowing you will never have a burger again?" The answer is: I am a person who thrives on happiness in the moment. And if I am happy with each meal I eat, I will continue to be happy, living from each wonderful moment to the next. My food makes me happy, healthy, and content. Nothing could ever taste better than that!

Just relax and remember: The plants are perfect so we don't have to be.

Come Join Me in the 13%

I am a proud graduate of the T. Colin Campbell Center for Nutrition Studies at Cornell University. While taking the Plant-Based Nutrition Certificate Program through the T. Colin Campbell Center for Nutrition Studies, I learned that, according to their research, there are more than 24,000 prescription and over-the-counter medicines registered in the United States. That number is alarming. If you go to your doctor with something that ails you, you are more than likely to leave with a prescription for medication or a suggestion for an over-the-counter drug.

Another alarming fact that I learned during my studies with the T. Colin Campbell Center for Nutrition Studies is that once Americans reach the age of fifty, 76% say they are taking at least one prescription drug on a regular basis. When Americans hit age sixty-five, 87% are taking a daily medication. I don't know about you, but I would rather be in the 13% living medication-free.

According to the T. Colin Campbell Center for Nutrition Studies, on average, people aged forty-five and older say they take four prescription medications daily. Between 1986 and 2002, Americans aged forty-five and older reported their regular use of prescription drugs increased from 52% to 75%.

The standard American diet has the odds stacked against us for good, long-term, medication-free health. The good news is—yes, there is good news—you can make a change in your own numbers and health issues through a whole-food, plant-based lifestyle. Will you join me in the 13%? Will you be the American who, like me, makes plans to be medication-free well into their sixties and beyond? This is why I eat this way every day. I enjoy my food and give myself the gift of knowing that by living this way I am dramatically decreasing the chances of me getting diseases that can be prevented through plants.

My cookbook has more than sixty recipes to inspire you to eat more plants. Think of plants in a positive way, and think of ways you can add more to each plate you eat from. I will give you all the recipes that you need to start a plant-based lifestyle. How do creamy soups, burgers, chili, dreamy cheesy dishes, all plant-based, sound to you? How does the idea of quick, easy cleanup sound to you?

I have been blessed to teach hundreds of people in my kitchen, but I can't possibly bring everyone into my home. The purpose of this book is to bring the Plant to Plate message of health to you.

This book will give you a great start to exploring the world of taking care of your health through food. I hope to share with you how to stop the struggle with dieting, how you can eat to live and eat for pleasure. Perhaps like me, no matter what you've tried, the weight won't come off or stay off. These recipes can help you to move forward.

I will also discuss exercise, sleep, what you need in your kitchen, and tips for grocery shopping. Eating plant-based can bring you great energy and great skin. Sometimes people even tell me I seem to be aging in reverse! I look back at photos from a few years ago, and I can say that I do look older in them than I do today.

Another important message I want to share with you is: Be kind to yourself. The plants are perfect so we don't have to be. If you find yourself living a whole-food, plant-based lifestyle and you eat something that isn't necessarily going to give you the best health, just move on and make your next meal plant-based. There's no plant-based police out there looking to scold you. Just do your best to eat more plants.

"There are so many beautiful reasons to eat plants!"
~ Catherine Niggemeier,
Plant to Plate

Grocery Tips

We have all heard the importance of shopping the perimeter of the supermarket. I am here to tell you that I only agree with a portion of that statement. There are some other aisles that I spend time shopping in on my weekly stops to the market. If you think about your standard supermarket and how it is set up, you will see why I say I only buy a portion of that thinking. Follow along with me and I will give you a Plant to Plate grocery tour.

I teach this to clients—no matter the supermarket chain I am in, I shop the same way in each of them. I spend most of my time in the fresh produce section, buying fresh, local, and in-season fruits and vegetables, then I head over to the rice and bean aisle, then finish up in the frozen food section of the store.

Another upside to shopping the Plant to Plate way is the amount of money you can save once you eliminate meat, dairy, and eggs, which can be very costly for your wallet and, in the end, perhaps your health.

Fresh or Frozen

I am often asked if frozen fruits and vegetables are as good as fresh, and the answer is YES! Frozen produce is typically more nutrient dense than unfrozen produce, since it's flash frozen at its peak ripeness right up until you thaw it. The great thing about frozen fruits and vegetables is they become staples that you can always have on hand. They won't spoil like fresh produce can if you don't get around to making it right away. They are so healthy for you, too! Buying berries and frozen greens like spinach and broccoli to have on hand are a great way to ensure a healthy meal. I love adding frozen organic berries to my smoothies.

If you shop at large warehouse-type stores, you can really save yourself lots of money and time shopping because the big bags last a long time and they are always offered at a much better price than your standard supermarket. Having frozen vegetables on hand makes it easy to steam or no-oil sauté, and they can make for a great stir-fry served over your favorite rice. Take advantage of sales and stock up! You won't have to worry about it going bad.

A favorite "frozen" dish of mine is my berry stew. I heat some frozen berries in a small pot on the stove, sprinkle in a small amount of brown sugar, and top it with raw walnuts for a heart-healthy dessert or morning breakfast. Having plants, either fresh or frozen, on hand allows me to always have something I enjoy ready and available to eat.

Here is another tip: rather than throwing out food that is about to expire or go bad, cook it and refrigerate it so you get a few more days to eat it. Nothing pains me more than to throw produce away. Since changing to a whole-food, plant-based lifestyle, not only have I become more appreciative of the food I eat, I never throw anything away. The main reason is I make things everyone in my house enjoys, so it always gets eaten quickly.

But another reason food doesn't go to waste here in my home is because my thinking is: If I have taken the time and pride in preparing it, I should value it and never waste it. If, by chance, I have leftovers in the fridge, they often become the next morning's breakfast. I enjoy making big batches of hummus and making "sandwiches" with fresh tomato and sliced red onion on red cabbage leaves rather than bread for a great start to my day. It is all about changing your thinking. Food is fuel and food is meant to be enjoyed. I have changed the way I define a good breakfast. Once I removed my thinking about certain foods that I considered breakfast-only foods, my options became greater and my health improved. As I type this, I am fueled by the big plate of lentils I had for breakfast. You can't find a better protein than that to start your day off right.

Stay Focused and Organized

Clients tell me they hate food shopping because it is so expensive or that it takes too long. Shopping the Plant to Plate way will not only save you money, it will save you time.

Three aisles. That's it. That is all you need to cover in a supermarket. Most stores are set up so that the produce is in the front of the store. I always make my way there first, then go to the rice, bean, and spice aisle, and finish up in frozen foods. As you quickly walk from one end of the store to the other, take note of the bright primary colors "food-like products" are packaged in. Food companies are doing their best to replicate the colors of plants. Take note of the bright red, purple, yellow, and orange packaging you see throughout the store. All that effort and design to attract you, yet all of the plants in the produce aisle already come in their own ready-to-eat-packages. Just peel and eat. Nothing can be more convenient than that.

The next time you are tempted to buy packaged foods, take a look at the sodium and sugar content. Every four grams of sugar a "food-like product" contains is equal to one teaspoon of sugar. I won't list any particular offenders, but really take a look at what is in most of what you find in the other aisles of the supermarket. Once you engage in this way of thinking about what you are putting in your cart and what you recognize to be real food, it can make all the difference in your shopping habits and can lead to better health.

This is not a difficult thing to do once you start to focus on real food. Eating plants does not have to be expensive. Set a budget for what you want to spend and stick to it. The benefits of eating healthy are priceless.

I will say it again: time spent in the supermarket is far better than time spent in the doctor's office or in line at the pharmacy. The amount of time spent in the kitchen preparing simple, plant-based ingredients is better than time spent on the phone with insurance companies waiting for approvals for testing. It most certainly beats waking up with aches and pains.

Food is the best way we can help our health, but it can also be the worst way to harm our health. If you approach the grocery store with a list of plants that you need as your weekly stock, you will be more likely to stick to a plan and build a standard of healthy food. Yes, there is some planning that goes into it, but once you find your go-to staples, it becomes easy to do.

So get your pen and paper ready, make a list, grab your recyclable bags, and head off to your market for the best plants you can buy!

Exercise

While I could list all the important things that exercise does for your body—and believe me, there are many—exercise alone cannot truly help you lose weight until you focus on good, nutritious food. Plant-based foods are the most nutritious for your health, and the best part is there is no need to practice portion control. Plants are filling and satisfying.

I quickly realized after a week of eating plant-based that the afternoon slump and hunger that I had always experienced were gone. I was no longer eating a mid-afternoon snack of high-protein, low-fat cheese or some other kind of food I thought would be beneficial to weight loss—I was eating less and moving more. I found myself with so much energy that taking a second walk in the same day with my golden retriever, Darby, became commonplace.

What Works For Me

I have always loved being outside in nature and walking. I would walk for miles a day while trying to lose weight, sadly to no avail. I would easily walk five miles a day during my attempts to drop the pounds. I took any opportunity to walk somewhere rather than take my car. For years, I would walk to the supermarket, the post office, the library, and with my daughters to school, even though their bus stop was at the end of our driveway. I loved walking to the elementary school with the girls, and I miss it so much today, but even with all of those added steps, it did not get me to my weight-loss goals.

Now, don't get me wrong, I know exercise is good for my mental and physical health, but it was not helping me lose weight. Once I started a whole-food, plant-based lifestyle, the weight came off, plain and simple. Food is the catalyst for weight loss, and exercise is the perfect partner to it. Once I started a whole-food, plant-based lifestyle, my energy increased and I felt fantastic. I began to walk faster as my weight dropped off, and exercise became something I did for pleasure rather than something I had to do. Eating plants made me feel better in all aspects of my life. I was waking up earlier and exercising earlier and feeling more productive during my day.

Exercise should be something you enjoy; it should not be a chore. It should be something that makes you feel great physically and mentally. My suggestion is this: do what you like and keep focused on what the exercise you do can do for your health. Sitting for long periods of time and being sedentary does not promote good health. If you are commuting to work, sitting in your car, then sitting at your desk all day, a brisk walk of thirty minutes is something that you can give yourself in the middle of the day. Approach exercise as a gift of health that you are giving yourself rather than something that has to be done.

Find an exercise that you enjoy and practice it daily. For me, it's a daily walk. I don't need a recovery day from walking, and I love being out in the fresh air, fueling my metabolism. This helps me manage my weight loss by keeping my muscles strong and blood pumping to my heart.

Walking helps to strengthen my bones and muscles. I have been a walker for more than two decades, and I was plenty surprised at the shape of my legs once I started to lose the weight. This is one of the first places I noticed a difference in my physical transformation. I did think that all those years of walking without weight loss were in vain, but really, my muscles and bones were thanking me under all that weight.

The best thing about walking is that you don't need any kind of equipment, special clothing (although I do have an obsession with hot-pink sneakers), or an appointment. Just go!

Just Move

Remember this: Bodies in motion stay in motion; bodies at rest stay at rest. Just move. As I write this, I am working from my standing desk. It has been the best thing I did for myself while writing my cookbook. Since I had changed my lifestyle and diet, I wasn't used to sitting down for long periods of time, so buying the desk has worked wonders for me. I realized that I needed one when my lower back started hurting, and I finally made

the connection that I was sitting for way too many hours at a time.

Why should you make time for movement? Have you heard that sitting is the new smoking? We all know how bad smoking is, so after hearing that, I knew I had to get up and move away from my desk. Plus, walking is fun! I love to spend time in New York City. Finding new places to walk allows me to go and explore while doing great things for my health.

Even if you can't get a standing desk, make it a priority to get up and *move* and walk around. You are entitled to it. You *deserve* to move around. If people can be given time for a smoke break, you can give yourself a healthy break and move. Go outside and walk.

Did you know that unhealthy employees are one of the most cost-draining factors for companies? Tell your management that you want to be healthier, using the argument that it will save them money. See if they'd be open to investing in a standing desk so that you spend less of your day being sedentary. By standing and getting breaks to move your body, you improve your health and their bottom line. I have worked with clients who have done this, and they have told me how they have seen changes in their overview of being healthy and in their posture, too! Tell me you didn't just sit up straight reading that last line! A happy, healthy employee is a cost-effective one.

You are worth it. You deserve good health. Think about how you want to feel later on in life. Get up and move, and continue to move so that you can always be able to move. Eating plants is the way I healed myself, and exercise is the plant-based cherry on top of my good health!

If you are exercising already, that's great! If you are not, consult with your doctor before starting any kind of exercise program to make sure you are in good health to do so. But in my opinion, at the end of the day it comes down to this for weight loss: It's the food, it's the food, it's the food! Eat more plants!

Dining Out

A healthy kitchen is a healthy you, but you may not eat dinner in your kitchen every night. Here are some tips for dining out.

Most people are shocked when I tell them I can eat anywhere, but I have yet to come across a restaurant where I can't find something to eat. I am always pleased when I don't get the question I often hear: "Catherine, can you eat here?" It makes me laugh, as if I would have my plant-based membership revoked if I walked into a restaurant that didn't serve anything but vegan fare. Just because food is labeled vegan does not mean it is healthy. Don't forget: Oreos are vegan, and they are far from healthy.

So what do you do if you are with other people who chose the restaurant? Have no fear, because you can do really well eating out whole-food, plant-based, even at a steak house.

Starters

First off, telling the waiter that you are plant-based and asking what they suggest may not always be the best route. Many times, people are confused about the meaning of plant-based, and it can give the waitstaff too much pressure and be off-putting. Instead, I suggest you take a good, long look at the menu and see what they have in their dishes. Look at a menu as an ingredients list and create your meal from what they have in other dishes.

For example, if you are in your standard American-cuisine restaurant and they serve nachos, you can look for guacamole and beans as two ingredients to create a meal around. Look for baked potatoes—most restaurants carry them as an option. Now you've built yourself a little potato bar with healthy, plant-based options. Pair a meal like this with a great big salad. I always ask for everything to be brought together at once so I can take my time and enjoy it as one big meal.

Sometimes when I eat out with others, I order my food and there will be a bit of a giggle from my tablemates about what I ordered. But once the meal comes, the comments are usually the same. "Wow, Catherine, that looks so good. I should have gotten that!"

It helps that I find joy in the company I am with and joy in the food I fuel my body with. I can remember all too well that overstuffed feeling I would always get before I changed to eating for health. Now when I eat out, I walk out of the restaurant feeling satisfied, light, and not bloated. Yes, it may take a few minutes more for me to order than others, but like I said, it's time I would rather spend making decisions for my health than in the doctor's waiting room.

I have cooked for more than a thousand people, so I know it's not an easy task to feed people. When ordering off-menu, remember that a smile goes a long way. Be polite, and don't assume they know what you want. Take a look at the menu ahead of time so you can already have an idea of what you would like, and more than likely, you will receive the service you expect.

Here are some of my favorite types of restaurants and what I order.

Italian

Oftentimes, Italian restaurants add Parmesan cheese to every dish. This is where I take time with the waitstaff to tell them I don't eat cheese and to please make sure my meal is made without it. Here are some of my favorites I often find in Italian restaurants: grilled vegetables, olives, pizza with grilled vegetables minus the cheese, pasta fagioli, escarole and beans, lentil soup, pastas, marinara sauce, minestrone, and bread.

One of my favorite dishes to order is angel hair spaghetti with garlic and lemon and topped with spinach. It is a fresh and light dish I created off a menu one night while out with friends. Guess what? They all asked to try it and loved it!

Greek

Oh, the list is endless in a Greek restaurant! Greek salads minus the feta cheese, olives, grilled vegetables, roasted vegetables, lemon rice, chickpea salad, falafel (check to see if it is made without egg), and grilled potatoes. The possible combinations in Greek restaurants are endless, and they're one of my favorite types of places to eat.

Chinese

This is possibly one of the best kinds of places to eat. Avoid all those fried, heavily sauced dishes and stick to the basics. There are so many great options! My go-to favorite is steamed rice with steamed vegetables. Now again, you might think that sounds boring, but it's not. Good health can't be boring. Get a side of soy sauce and hot mustard and create your own combination of sauces for a flavorful dish of good health. Steamed vegetable dumplings and vegetable soups are another great healthy option.

Mexican

The one thing to watch in a Mexican restaurant when eating for health is the lard that is typically found in most of their dishes. Win your waitstaff over, and then ask them to prepare your dish without lard. Rice, guacamole, vegetable tacos, and vegetable fajitas are all great options. I always ask for extra limes to squeeze over my dish to bring out all the flavors.

Go out and try something new! Most restaurants offer their menus online, and it's a great tool to get a sense of what they offer. Once you get started dining out plant-based, remember that you are eating for health, and put that as your top priority when ordering. Once health becomes your focus, you will become a pro at dining out!

Sleep

Sleep was something I struggled with, my last unhealthy holdout that I worked on every night. Sometimes the night just crept up so fast. If you are like me and have a busy household, day-to-day life is full of lots of running around with kids, after-school sports, and helping with homework, so getting to bed at a healthy time can be a challenge. When I make a conscious effort to be in bed by 10 p.m., it sets me up for the best health the next day. When I stray from that, the next day can be a challenge, so I do my best to honor my health by getting to bed at a healthy time each night.

When I started a whole-food, plant-based lifestyle, one of the first things I noticed was how energized I became. I would rise by 5:15 a.m., an hour earlier than I did prior to becoming plant-based.

Waking at 6:15 used to give me enough time to get up and take my daughters to school, but I was not working at the time, so I thought it was a good enough time to wake up. Yet I couldn't wake from my dead, sluggish sleep without the sound of my loud, obnoxious alarm clock. When I think back to it, that was such a horrible, jarring way to start the day! Compared to how I wake up now, energized and ready to go and to take on the day, there's no debate in which I prefer. I can recall feeling achy when I woke and not as clear-headed as I do now. I enjoy the morning so much better and appreciate the new day ahead. Waking up now feels gentle and kind, not grueling and uncomfortable as it did before.

Here are some tips that I incorporated to give myself the best health through sleep.

Just like food, if I don't create healthy habits around sleep, I won't honor my health in the best way I can.

Setting my room up for good sleep requires that my room temperature be at sixty-six degrees. I live in a 100-year-old house with amazing cast-iron radiators that really holds the heat well. If I have not turned down the heat before bed, I know I will not have good rest, so this is something I make sure I do. Again, my health is a priority, so I make sure I do what I can to ensure the best sleep.

I am forty-nine, and I no longer wake in the middle of the night and encounter waves of hot flashes like I did before changing my diet. My food is so gentle on my system that it never interrupts my good sleep—just another upside to whole-food, plant-based living.

Consider sleeping with your blinds or curtains open. I personally love the moonlight coming through the windows at night, as this makes for a peaceful rest. Then, come morning, what better way to rise than the sun shining in? It is a simple gift I give myself to wait and watch for it coming through my window. Plant-based living has made me more thankful and aware of everything in my life, including sunrises and sunsets.

Because I am so active during the day, sleep is a welcomed gift at the end of the day. The foods I eat promote good sleep, and because I have so much energy, I no longer drink coffee, which in the past disrupted my sleep patterns. I find that because of my healthy eating habits, I can achieve a deeper sleep and an easy rising. Eventually I became so programmed in my routine that I was able to remove the alarm clock from my room. Once I attained healthy sleep, waking up became so much simpler.

Next, consider removing the television from your bedroom and keeping all electronics somewhere else at night. When my daughter received her first smartphone at fourteen, we made a house rule: no phones in the bedroom, so that she could get good rest. Of course, as a parent, if you are preaching good habits to your kids, it's a hard sell for them to buy if you are not doing it yourself, so in the end, having a fourteen-year-old with a smartphone turned out to be a good thing!

Keep bedtime consistent. I don't let my bedtime routine change all that much just because it's the weekend. There are times that I will stay out later when socializing, but it doesn't take me too long to realize the next day why healthy sleep is so important. When I sleep well, I am well. Oftentimes I will post a positive message on my Instagram and Facebook page about good sleep, and I hear feedback such as "thanks for the reminder, I need to get more rest." Like I always tell clients, the plants are perfect so we don't have to be. Nothing can be perfect all the time, but we can work to perfect things in our life that will give us better health.

Good sleep and good rest is something to be proud of. So many people take pride in saying that they don't require much sleep or that they can sleep when they die. If you feel like you are dying during the day and you are run down and using sugar and/or caffeine to make it through, consider giving yourself good, healthy sleep and see what happens. Your body and mind will thank you. I found myself working more efficiently when I incorporated healthy sleep patterns into my life.

If you are reading this book in bed, put it down. I wish sweet, plant-based dreams to you!

"Dream about plants and have the best night's sleep!"
~ Catherine Niggemeier, Plant to Plate

Pantry

One of the great things about whole-food, plant-based living are the seasons. Do your best to go with local, organic, in-season foods. Why? When food is grown closer to us, it is better for us. With every season, there is variety, a new and amazing vegetable for us to try.

Frozen fruits and vegetables are a mainstay as well, because I can't imagine not having access to berries and I am so thankful for the frozen stock in my freezer. My kitchen is simple and easy to maintain so that I can always make satisfying, filling, and healthy meals quickly! I love organization and order in my life, and knowing that I always have my go-to items adds order and happiness to my life.

Here are a few of my must-haves in my plant-based kitchen.

Vegetables (fresh or frozen)	Fruits (fresh or frozen)	Herbs and Spices	Raw Nuts and Seeds
Baby spinach	Apples	Basil (fresh or dry)	Almonds
Bell peppers	Avocado	Bay leaves (dry)	Cashews
Broccoli	Bananas	Black pepper	Peanuts
Carrots	Blackberries	Chili powder	Pecans
Cauliflower	Cantaloupe	Cinnamon	
Celery	Coconut	Crushed red pepper	Chia seeds
Corn	Cranberries	Fine salt	Ground flaxseed
Garlic	Cucumbers	Garlic powder	Ground tahini paste
Italian flat-leaf parsley	Dates	Ground cumin	Pumpkin seeds
Kale	Grapes	Kosher salt	Sunflower seeds
Leeks	Kiwi	Nutmeg	
Onions	Mangoes	Onion powder	Whole Grains and Flours
Potatoes (russet and sweet)	Olives	Oregano (dry)	Barley
Red-leaf cabbage	Oranges	Paprika	Brown rice
Romaine lettuce	Pears	Rosemary (fresh or dry)	Bulgur
White cabbage	Pineapple	Tarragon (dry)	Farro
	Raspberries	Turmeric	Israeli couscous
	Strawberries		Quinoa
	Tomatoes		Rolled oats
	Watermelon		
			Almond meal
			Chickpea flour
			Popcorn kernels
			Unbleached all-purpose flour

Ditching Dairy

I really believe in my message of plant positivity, and I do my best to encourage people to eat more plants without sounding negative. But when it comes to the importance of ditching dairy, I realize sometimes that I border on the stronger side.

Please do your best for yourself and your family to drop cow's milk from your home. The main purpose for cow's milk is to grow a baby calf to a full-grown, thousand-pound cow. Think about that, and we don't have to wonder why obesity is at an all-time high in the U.S.

Cheese is on *everything*, and cheese is made from cow secretions: milk! Yes, I said secretions. Think of it that way, and you may move faster away from cow's milk and cow's milk products. I believed for too long that dairy was the protein I needed to get myself thin—it's not true! I firmly believe that ditching dairy is a key part of attaining long-term health and weight loss.

There are a variety of plant-based cheeses becoming more and more available at local supermarkets. While highly processed, if it gets you to stop eating dairy products, then be adventurous and try some. In the meantime, here are a list of plant-based items you can enjoy. Don't forget to try my recipe for Plant to Plate 7-Minute Almond Milk listed on pg. 41.

Almond milk   Cashew milk
Coconut milk

Here is a list of plant-based, nut-free alternatives to cow's milk dairy. You may find cheeses and milks made from these plants.

Flax milk	Hemp milk
Oat milk	Pumpkin seed milk
Quinoa milk	Rice milk
Soy milk	Sunflower seed milk

Satisfying Your Sweet Tooth

Remember sugar is sugar, so always use sparingly. Here are some plant-based suggestions to add sweetness to a dish:

Agave syrup	Brown sugar
Coconut sugar	Maple syrup
Organic cane sugar	

Oils

I can't stress this enough: oil is not a health food and is highly processed. Did you know that it takes twenty-three olives to make one tablespoon of olive oil? I don't know about you, but I would rather eat twenty-three olives than waste a tablespoon of olive oil for sautéing.

Think of it this way: Do you really taste the olive oil in foods that you sauté? I don't! You will see throughout this book, I never sauté in oil. Do your best to avoid oils in your cooking. One tablespoon of olive oil is 120 calories, so think next time before you pour some in your pan. Every year there will be the next healthy oil marketed to us, but remember that oils are not a health food.

Broths

If you can make you own, wonderful! If you are like me, a busy business owner, wife, and mother, I always have low-sodium vegetable broth on hand. It is my go-to for sautéing and for adding to soups and stews.

Beans and Legumes

Oh, how I love beans and legumes! They are fantastic! They are low in cost, filled with fiber, heart healthy, low in fat, packed with protein, satisfying, versatile, loaded with nutrients, and always on hand in my pantry.

Yes, it is said that soaking your beans is better for you, and I agree, but I am a busy woman, and I never want to be stuck not having beans ready to go. Having BPA-free canned beans in my pantry allows me to make a quick, nutritious meal for myself and my family.

A few of my favorites:

Black beans	Blackeyes
Cannellini beans	Chickpeas
French lentils	Green lentils
Kidney beans	Navy beans
Pinto beans	Split peas

Breads and Pasta

Black-bean-flour pasta
Chickpea-flour pasta
Corn tortillas
Lentil-flour pasta
Sourdough bread
Whole-grain, fresh-sprouted Ezekial bread
Whole-wheat pasta, assorted shapes and sizes
Whole-wheat tortillas

Plant-based Freezer Foods

Frozen strawberries   Frozen blackberries
Frozen raspberries   Frozen pineapple
Frozen cherries   Frozen cranberries
Frozen peas   Frozen corn
Frozen broccoli   Frozen spinach
Ezekial bread
Plant to Plate Bean Burgers (pg. 93)
Plant to Plate Pesto (pg. 50)
Plant to Plate Lentil Meatballs (pg. 99)
Pizza dough
Whole-grain waffles

Miscellaneous Items

Nutritional yeast is the only ingredient in my cookbook that you may have not heard of, but it is a fantastic addition to any plant-based kitchen.

First, what is it? Nutritional yeast is deactivated yeast that comes in a powder or flake. My favorite brand that I buy at my local health food store, Cornucopia, is the Frontier brand, and I believe you can buy this item online. Nutritional yeast is loaded with B-complex vitamins, including B12. It doesn't taste like yeast, and it can add a nutty, cheesy, creamy flavor to your dishes. Try my recipe for Spaghetti Carbonara on (pg. 104), which calls for nutritional yeast.

Vegan Butter

My favorite brand of vegan butter is Earth's Balance. Before you think I am contradicting myself in regards to processed foods, yes, vegan butter is processed, but it's not made from cream from a cow. And it is used very sparingly in my home. The great thing is both of my girls were fine with the switch, so I was happy to have one more item in my refrigerator made from plants.

Vegan Chocolate

This is something I do not use very often, but sometimes life needs a little chocolate. I always have a bag on hand in the pantry. I use these for two of my recipes if the mood strikes for a little chocolate taste: Plant to Plate Apple Nachos (pg. 116) and Plant to Plate Cookie Clusters (pg. 119). I love making these two recipes for my daughters' friends because most kids like the idea of eating something sweet, and when they realize it doesn't come from a package or a box, they seem to enjoy it even more!

Enjoy Life vegan chocolate is free of dairy, nuts, soy, gluten, wheat, tree nuts, and casein.

Plant-based Egg Substitute

MAKES EQUIVALENT OF 1 EGG

Flax seed meal and water act just like an egg, as they are both binders and add moisture to recipes. Flax seed is free of cholesterol and full of omega-3 and omega-6 fats, which add powerful benefits to your overall health. Use this quick little recipe as an egg substitute!

1   tablespoon ground flax seed
3   tablespoons water

1. Mix ingredients well and chill in fridge for 15 minutes.

"Eat more plants. The best is yet to come!"
~ Catherine Niggemeier, Plant to Plate

"Stress less, eat plants!"
~ Catherine Niggemeier,
Plant to Plate

Kitchen Tools

I am not much of a gadget person, but here are some essential tools for a plant-based kitchen:

A set of sharp knives. Although they can be expensive, it is worth the lifetime investment. Like I always say, I would rather pay for preventative care than medicines, so similarly, the price of a good knife is worth it to me in the long run.

Assorted pots and pans. Sauté pans, a large stockpot, and lidded saucepans are key tools for cooking in a plant-based kitchen. Also important is a small pot with a lid to heat up leftovers. I do not have a microwave in my home, so a small pot is the best tool for heating food up very quickly. I love my Le Creuset Dutch oven for soups, chilis, and stews.

Machinery. My Cuisinart food processor is my go-to for hummus, pesto, and desserts—all easily made in this wonderful, small kitchen appliance. While I am not a paid spokesperson for Vitamix, I can't talk about this high-speed blender enough. I have owned mine for more than seven years and it is just amazing! I make smoothies, soups, nut cheeses, and so many other healthy recipes in my Vitamix. It is a worthy investment in good health!

Small tools and boards. A large cutting board is very handy for chopping up all those wonderful fresh fruits and vegetables. Use half-sheet pans for roasting delicious vegetables and baked goods. A Microplane grater is fantastic for zesting citrus or grating garlic, nutmeg, or vegan chocolate.

Other small tools to have: a hand-held citrus squeezer, spatulas, whisks, and wooden spoons.

Glass containers for leftovers and storage. No plastic containers! Drop the plastic from your kitchen and switch to glass. Your food will look more appealing and be free of chemicals that can leach into your food. During my cooking classes, I often have clients ask to see my fridge, and they tell me that everything looks so inviting because they can see everything. Try some glass containers and see how inviting your plant-based food looks.

Large glass mixing bowls. Use these for creating large salads that can be the focal point at every meal.

Nut-milk bag. A key tool for making Plant to Plate 7-Minute Almond Milk (pg. 41).

Unbleached parchment paper. This makes cleanup easier when roasting vegetables or beans or baking cookies.

Liquid Love— Drinks and Smoothies

The beautiful thing about frozen fruits is that we can enjoy them all year round. I don't think I could make it through the winter without the enjoyment of berries and pineapple.

You will notice that every smoothie recipe starts with a healthy handful of kale. I use triple-washed baby kale so there is no need for me to prep or stem the kale. I like everything to be simple and fast, and triple-washed kale does the job!

But why kale? I love greens in everything I make. The beauty of kale, unlike spinach, is you will not taste the kale in any of my smoothie recipes. Kale is low in calories, high in fiber, and has no fat. Kale has become this cool, hip food to eat, and I couldn't agree more. Kale is one of the healthiest and most nutritious foods you can eat. Being healthy is cool, living medication-free is cool, and living a long, healthy, and energized life couldn't be any cooler in my eyes.

Blending tip: It's very important to blend the kale first, then add the remaining ingredients, unless you enjoy chewing your smoothies. If you *do* enjoy chewing your smoothies, you'll get no judgment from me. Chew away!

Plant to Plate
7-Minute Almond Milk

MAKES 1 QUART

Yes! I call this 7-minute almond milk because that is the time it takes to make from start to finish! This recipe is made very quickly with a high-speed Vitamix blender. If you do not have a high-speed blender, soak the almonds for a minimum of 3 hours or overnight to make the blending process easier.

Plant-based milk is pure and clean and free of hormones and animal secretions and can be the perfect pairing with my recipe for plant-based cookies!

- 1 cup raw almonds
- 4 cups water
- 1 teaspoon vanilla
  Pinch of salt

1. Place all ingredients in blender and whip until fully blended.

2. Pour blended mixture through a nut-milk bag into a large glass bowl. This will separate the liquid almond milk from the almond pulp.

3. Squeeze the remaining liquid from the bag so you don't waste any of your delicious almond milk.

4. Funnel into a glass bottle or jar and refrigerate.

5. Serve well chilled.

6. Enjoy in the best of health!

Plant to Plate
Berry Bliss Smoothie

MAKES 2 SMOOTHIES

How can you resist trying something with the word bliss in the title? This smoothie is refreshing and enjoyable and loaded with antioxidants. Take one sip and you'll understand the name.

- 1 cup triple-washed baby kale
- 1-1/2 cups mixed frozen berries
- 1 cup water or 1 cup Plant to Plate 7-Minute Almond Milk or any plant-based milk you enjoy
- 1 tablespoon agave syrup (optional)
- 1 freshly squeezed lemon

1. Blend the kale and water until the kale is in liquid form. Don't forget this very important first step or you will end up with a chewy smoothie!

2. Combine all ingredients in a high-speed blender. Blend on high until smooth, adding more liquid if needed to get the consistency you desire.

3. Enjoy in the best of health!

"Plant positivity, health positivity,
life positivity!"
~ Catherine Niggemeier,
Plant to Plate

Plant to Plate Watermelon Kale Heaven Smoothie

MAKES 2 SMOOTHIES

I call this my Heaven Smoothie because I imagine that heaven will be this good!

- 1 cup triple-washed baby kale
- 1 cup water
- 2 cups fresh watermelon, cubed
- 1 freshly squeezed lime
- 1 cup fresh strawberries
- 1/2 cup frozen berries

1. Blend the kale and water until the kale is in liquid form. Don't forget this very important first step or you will end up with a chewy smoothie!

2. Add remaining ingredients and blend on high until smooth, adding more liquid if needed to get the consistency you desire.

3. Enjoy in the best of health!

Plant to Plate Pineapple Punch Smoothie

MAKES 2 SMOOTHIES

Yes, I have a true love affair with pineapple. This smoothie really hits the spot on a hot day! I only use and recommend fresh or frozen pineapple for this!

- 1 cup triple-washed baby kale
- 1 cup water
- 2 cups fresh pineapple
  Zest of 1 orange
- 1/2 cup orange juice
- 1/2 freshly squeezed lemon

1. Blend the kale and water until the kale is in liquid form.

2. Add remaining ingredients and blend on high until smooth, adding more liquid if needed to get the consistency you desire.

3. Enjoy in the best of health!

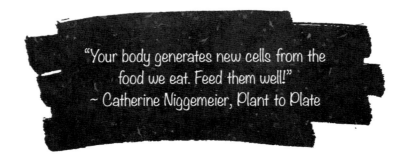
"Your body generates new cells from the food we eat. Feed them well!"
~ Catherine Niggemeier, Plant to Plate

"Good things happen
when you eat plants!"
~ Catherine Niggemeier,
Plant to Plate

Plant to Plate Cheerful Cherry Smoothie

MAKES 2 SMOOTHIES

The beauty of this little smoothie is that you can make it on the thicker side by using less water and enjoy it like a frozen dessert minus the added sugar and other interesting ingredients found in most frozen store-bought desserts.

- 1 cup triple-washed baby kale
- 1 cup water
- 2 cups frozen cherries
- 1 apple, seeded and cored
- 1 lime, zest and juice

1. Blend the kale and water until the kale is in liquid form.

2. Add remaining ingredients and blend on high until smooth, adding liquid to get the consistency you desire.

3. Enjoy in the best of health!

Plant to Plate Apple Cleanse Smoothie

MAKES 2 SMOOTHIES

Apples are great for weight loss. They keep you full, are loaded with fiber, can help to lower your cholesterol, and can boost your immune system.

- 1 cup triple-washed baby kale
- 1 cup water
- 2 apples, seeded and cored
- 1 lemon, zest and juice
- 2 large carrots

1. Blend the kale and water until the kale is in liquid form.

2. Add remaining ingredients and blend on high until smooth, adding liquid to get the consistency you desire.

3. Enjoy in the best of health!

"When food shopping, buying plants compared to buying animal proteins will be much kinder to your wallet and your health!"
~ Catherine Niggemeier, Plant to Plate

Plant to Plate Heavenly Avacado Spread, pg. 55

Dressings, Dips, and Sauces! Flavor, Flavor, Flavor!

When I made the change to a whole-food, plant-based lifestyle, I quickly realized that my old way of eating was so bland and my food lacked the natural, robust flavor that I now enjoy at every meal. The following dressings, dips, and sauces are a great addition to so many meals.

Do you know that even the people who tell me that they could never eat the way I eat love my recipes, especially my oil-free hummus? You will see throughout my book that all of my recipes contain everyday ingredients that you know. How great is that? I promise you, you won't have to travel to far-off exotic lands to find the ingredients. A quick trip to the market is all you need.

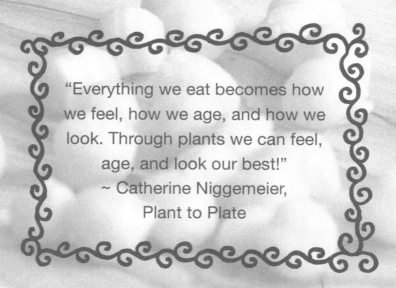

"Everything we eat becomes how we feel, how we age, and how we look. Through plants we can feel, age, and look our best!"
~ Catherine Niggemeier,
Plant to Plate

Hannah's Plant to Plate Hummus

MAKES 2 CUPS

Steve and I have always loved hummus. We have been making hummus since we got married nineteen years ago. We knew it was delicious, but we never realized back then how much healthier we could make it. Hummus is traditionally made with olive oil, but olive oil adds unnecessary calories and fat, so in my recipe I omit any added oil.

This is a great recipe that we use in so many different ways—as a salad topper, a bagel spread, a baked-potato stuffing, veggie dip, and all-around party pleaser.

- 1 can chickpeas, drained, liquid reserved
- 2 cans chickpeas, drained and rinsed
- 3 cloves garlic
- 3 tablespoons tahini
  Juice of 1 lemon
  Salt and pepper to taste

1. In a food processor, mince the garlic.

2. Add in the 3 cans of rinsed and drained chickpeas, tahini, lemon, salt, and pepper. Blend until smooth.

3. To get a creamy consistency, slowly add in the reserved chickpea juice to your desired consistency.

4. Enjoy in the best of health!

Plant to Plate Guacamole

MAKES 3 CUPS

If you enjoy making guacamole as much as I do in the Plant to Plate kitchen, consider investing in a molcajete. The Mexican version of the mortar and pestle, this tool is made from volcanic rock and gains a seasoned flavor over time. The more you use it, the more flavorful your guacamole becomes.

- 1/4 sweet onion, finely diced
- 2 cloves garlic, minced
  Juice of 1 lemon
  Salt and pepper to taste
- 3 ripe avocados

1. In a bowl or molcajete, mash the onion, garlic, lemon juice, salt, and pepper into a wet paste.

2. Slice and pit the avocado and scoop out the flesh and add to the paste. Mix well with the tines of a fork. Add more salt to season as desired.

3. Chill and serve.

4. Enjoy in the best of health!

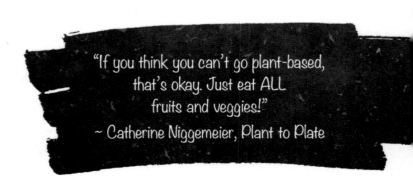

"If you think you can't go plant-based, that's okay. Just eat ALL fruits and veggies!"
~ Catherine Niggemeier, Plant to Plate

Plant to Plate Guacamole

Hannah's Plant to Plate Hummus

Plant to Plate Pesto

MAKES 2 CUPS

Because of my love of pesto, my garden is on full basil production every summer! I plant so much basil because I make up big batches and freeze so I can enjoy the amazing taste of summer basil that I love so much throughout the year. I think the combination of basil, walnuts, and garlic in this recipe is incredible!

Most pesto recipes use a lot of olive oil. Do you know that adding just 1/2 cup of olive oil to any recipe adds 960 calories to a typical dish? I never count calories, but when I began to eat for health, I truly saw the importance of making changes to the way I prepared my food.

4	cups fresh basil leaves
3	cloves garlic
3/4	cup walnuts
1	ripe avocado
1/4	cup low-sodium vegetable broth
	Salt and pepper to taste

1. Heat dry skillet on medium-high heat and toast walnuts for 5 minutes to release the flavor. In a food processor, blend the garlic, walnuts, and basil leaves.

2. Add the avocado to the food processor and blend, then slowly add the broth a little at a time, until you get a creamy consistency. Season with salt and pepper.

3. Once the batch is made, I split the recipe into batches and store in the freezer. I pull from the freezer as needed and enjoy it over fresh pasta, fresh zucchini noodles, sweet potato toast, or on sourdough toast.

4. Enjoy in the best of health!

Cooking tip: Don't get caught up in the traditional method of following recipes. Ditch the must-use or must-have-on-hand mentality. I take the stress out of cooking and do what is easiest and best for me.

The first time I realized this was the best way to cook was when I was making pesto. I didn't have pine nuts, but I did have walnuts. That's when I decided the walnuts would have to do, and that is how I created this recipe.

Walnuts are always on hand in my kitchen because they offer an excellent source of anti-inflammatory omega-3 fatty acids. Walnuts are also rich in antioxidants. Research shows that walnuts may support brain function and health.

"Take time to feed your heart well!"
~ Catherine Niggemeier,
Plant to Plate

Plant to Plate Healthy Heart Tomato Sauce

MAKES 2 QUARTS

If you take a moment to look at all the unnecessary ingredients found in jarred sauce, you can see why I make this quick and easy sauce for my family. Use it on top of fresh pasta or fresh, raw zucchini spirals.

One good reason why you should incorporate this heart-healthy tomato sauce into your weekly whole-food, plant-based repertoire is San Marzano tomatoes! These tomatoes are less acidic than other tomatoes and are loaded with flavor and anti-cancer benefits. The skin is thinner and makes for an easy, tasty bite. Tomatoes, like all plants, are great for your digestive health and your skin!

- 1 sweet onion, chopped
- 1 cup low-sodium vegetable broth, more as needed
- 3 cloves garlic
- 1 tablespoon Italian seasoning
- 1 teaspoon sugar
- 8 fresh basil leaves
- 2 28-ounce cans San Marzano whole tomatoes
- Salt and pepper to taste

1. In large pan on medium-high heat, sauté onion in low-sodium vegetable broth for 10 minutes until onion is very soft. Be careful not to burn it, adding more broth if needed.

2. Add minced garlic and the Italian seasoning and cook for another 3 minutes.

3. Cook until the liquid has been reduced, but do not dry out the pan or burn.

4. In a glass bowl, empty the tomatoes and the juice. With clean hands, crush the San Marzano tomatoes.

5. Add the tomatoes and juice to the pan, then the sugar and basil leaves. Stir well. Bring to a boil and then simmer for 30 minutes. Add salt and pepper to taste.

6. Enjoy in the best of health!

Plant to Plate Tahini Sauce

MAKES 1/2 CUP

Oh, how I love this dressing! It is so great for so many dishes. It's one of my go-to salad dressings and pairs really well with Plant to Plate Falafel (pg. 97) or Steve's Plant to Plate Bean Burgers (pg. 93).

- 1/4 cup tahini
- 2 teaspoons fresh lemon juice
- 2 cloves garlic, minced
- 2 tablespoons water
- 1/2 teaspoon salt

1. Place all ingredients into a bowl and whisk. If you want a thinner consistency, slowly add more water.

2. Enjoy in the best of health!

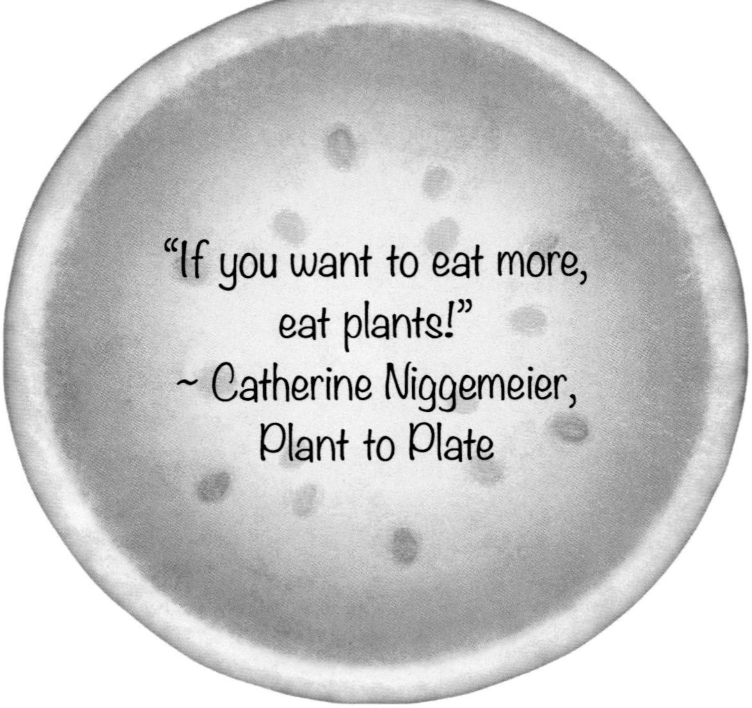

"If you want to eat more,
eat plants!"
~ Catherine Niggemeier,
Plant to Plate

Plant to Plate Heavenly Avocado Spread

MAKES 1/2 QUART

As you can tell by now, I like to call my recipes names like heaven, bliss, and joy, because that is how I truly think and feel about the food I make and serve to my family and clients! My family loves when I make this for a trip to the beach. We bring some of our favorite New York bagels or a hearty sourdough bread for sandwiches to be enjoyed by the ocean.

Double the recipe if serving a larger group, but keep in mind it is best served fresh. This doesn't hold up well for more than twenty-four hours in the refrigerator, so make for what you will eat at a sitting. This is definitely not a batch recipe!

1   can chickpeas, rinsed and drained
1   ripe small avocado
1/4   cup sunflower seeds
1   cup celery, diced
     Salt and pepper to taste

1. In large glass bowl, use a potato masher to mash the chickpeas to a chunky consistency.

2. In separate bowl, use the back of a fork to mash avocado into a smooth consistency (think of this as nature's mayonnaise).

3. Fold in the avocado, then add in celery, sunflower seeds, and salt and pepper to taste. Mix well.

4. Cover and chill for 30 minutes and serve.

5. Enjoy in the best of health!

"Buy food that doesn't require
an ingredients list!"
~ Catherine Niggemeier,
Plant to Plate

Plant to Plate
Love Dressing

MAKES 1-1/2 CUPS

This dressing can be added to any of your favorite salads or fresh raw veggies, giving you a big bowl of love. It is the perfect dressing for my Plant to Plate Broccoli Love Salad (pg. 82).

- 1 cup tahini
- 1/4 cup water
- 1/2 cup fresh lemon juice
- 1 teaspoon white wine vinegar
- 1/4 teaspoon Italian seasoning
- 2–3 cloves garlic, grated with microplane grater
- Salt and pepper to taste

1. Whisk all ingredients together until smooth, adding water in slowly. Add more as needed to get desired consistency.

2. Serve chilled.

3. Enjoy in the best of health!

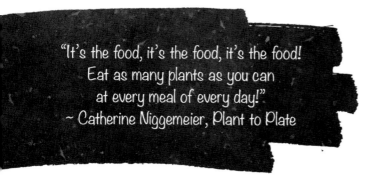

"It's the food, it's the food, it's the food!
Eat as many plants as you can
at every meal of every day!"
~ Catherine Niggemeier, Plant to Plate

Plant to Plate
Vinaigrette

MAKES 1/2 CUP

This dressing goes great with my Plant to Plate Lentil and Butternut Squash Salad (pg. 80) or any fresh raw greens that you enjoy! Plant power!

- Juice of 1 lemon
- 2 teaspoons Dijon mustard
- 1 tablespoon red wine vinegar
- 1/4 teaspoon Italian seasoning

1. Combine ingredients and whisk together.

2. Enjoy in the best of health!

Plant to Plate
Red Wine Vinaigrette

MAKES 1/2 CUP

This vinaigrette is light and adds great flavor to your plant-based dishes and pairs really well with Plant to Plate Orzo Salad (pg. 82). Once you become used to quickly whipping this dressing up, it can become your go-to dressing and will make store-bought salad dressing pale in comparison.

- 1/4 cup red wine vinegar
- 1 teaspoon Dijon mustard
- 1/2 teaspoon white sugar
- 1/2 teaspoon Italian seasoning
- Salt and pepper to taste

1. Whisk all ingredients together in a bowl.

2. Enjoy in the best of health!

"Learn to love fast food like
bananas, oranges, and apples!"
~ Catherine Niggemeier,
Plant to Plate

Steve's Plant to Plate Salad Dressing

MAKES 1/2 CUP

Yes, I give full credit to my main man, life partner, and kitchen mate for this one! This is a great dressing for so many things. We love this over arugula, fresh tomatoes, thinly sliced white onion, and sunflower seeds. You can use this dressing on any salad you create in your own kitchen. You don't need much to add a little bit of flavor to your salad.

Juice of 2 lemons
2 tablespoons Dijon mustard
1 tablespoon red wine vinegar
1 teaspoon white sugar
Salt and pepper to taste

1. Combine lemon juice, mustard, red wine vinegar, sugar, salt, and pepper.

2. Enjoy in the best of health!

Plant to Plate Oh My! Dressing

MAKES 1 CUP

Yes, that is the actual name of this dressing, because that is what everyone says after they have tried it. I love to use it on my bean burger or falafel recipes (you'll find them later in the book). Try adding it to a shredded coleslaw mix, too!

3 cloves garlic
1/2 cup tahini
1/4 cup water
Juice of 2 lemons
Salt and pepper to taste

1. Grate the garlic cloves with a Microplane grater into a mixing bowl.

2. Add in tahini, lemon juice, salt, and pepper and slowly whisk together, adding water to desired consistency.

3. Chill for at least one hour and serve.

4. Enjoy in the best of health!

"Remove artificially colored food from your plate and instead fill it with naturally colored plants."
~ Catherine Niggemeier, Plant to Plate

Plant to Plate Minestrone, pg. 67

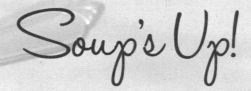

Soup's Up!

Oh, why do I love soups? Let me count the ways. First, there is something so lovely about a few simple ingredients coming together in one big pot. The satisfaction and simplicity of feeding myself and the ones I love with a big bowl of heartiness and health fills my plant-based heart.

Enjoying a healthy soup can assist in weight loss. How great is that? It's a double hit—you are filled and satisfied and you are being kind to your body.

Soup is a relatively inexpensive meal to put together. Most of my soups start with onion, celery, carrots, and garlic—very healthy and inexpensive ingredients.

Soup is a great way to batch cook for the week ahead. If you have soup in the fridge, you will never go hungry. Once you sit down to enjoy that big bowl of deliciousness, your hunger will be a thing of the past, and your desire for food will be more than satisfied.

Soup can be a family cooking event with children and make your process go faster. Most kids love to peel carrots and chop celery. This is a great way to teach your children how to take a few simple ingredients that will lead them to feeding themselves in an inexpensive way. It becomes their creation, something they can be proud of.

Give a child a bowl of soup, they will eat one hearty meal. Teach a child how to make soup, and they will never go hungry!

Plant to Plate
Chickpea Love Soup

MAKES 2 QUARTS

I call this Love Soup because one taste of it will cause you to fall in love with the flavor. There's no better way of loving yourself than eating soups like this one!

- 1   sweet onion
- 3   cloves garlic, minced
- 4   large carrots, diced
- 4   stalks celery, diced
- 1/2   cup low-sodium vegetable broth
- 2   tablespoons tomato paste
- 1   28-ounce can crushed tomatoes
- 2   teaspoons Italian seasoning
- 2   cans chickpeas, rinsed and drained
- 4   cups water
- 1-1/4   cup mini elbows or any other small pasta you like

1. In a large stockpot, sauté the onion, garlic, carrots, and celery in vegetable broth on medium-high heat until soft, approximately 10 minutes. Be careful not to burn the ingredients, adding more liquid as needed.

2. Add in tomato paste and Italian seasoning and sauté for another 3 minutes.

3. Add in crushed tomatoes, chickpeas, and water. Bring to a boil and simmer for 40 minutes.

4. Add in pasta and cook for an additional 8 minutes until pasta is al dente.

5. Enjoy in the best of health!

Plant to Plate
Favorite Potato Soup

MAKES 2 QUARTS

Comfort food is the best way to describe this delicious soup. What is more comforting than a big bowl of creamy potato soup on a cold winter day? The comfort of this soup in particular is knowing that potatoes provide us with the energy we need to perform our best. Potatoes have more potassium than a banana, and they are low in sodium and can reduce the risk of stroke.

Do not fear the potato or believe the hype that they will make you gain weight. Enjoy a potato today!

- 1   large onion, chopped
- 3   stalks celery, diced
- 3   carrots, diced
- 3   cloves garlic, minced
- 1   cup low-sodium vegetable broth
- 2   pounds russet potatoes, peeled and cut into 1-inch pieces
- 3   tablespoons dill
- 1   tablespoon salt
- 1   teaspoon pepper
- 4   cups water, using more or less for desired consistency
-     Salt and pepper to taste

1. In a large pot, sauté the onion, celery, carrots, and garlic in low-sodium vegetable broth until soft, approximately 10 minutes.

2. Add in potatoes, dill, salt, pepper, and water. Boil for 30 minutes or until potatoes are softened.

3. Carefully pour soup into blender (it's hot!) and puree for creamy consistency. If you want a chunky consistency, blend only half of the soup.

4. Enjoy in the best of health!

"Pay for your health in the produce aisle, not in the pharmacy aisle!"
~ Catherine Niggemeier, Plant to Plate

Plant to Plate
Chowder Time Soup

MAKES 6 SERVINGS

This ain't your typical chow-da! This is a healthy alternative that is free of creams, cholesterol, and oodles of calories. Don't worry, it's still loaded with flavor and creaminess, but this one won't hurt your health.

- 1   32-ounce box low-sodium vegetable broth
- 1   small onion, finely diced
- 3   cloves garlic, minced
- 3   medium carrots, diced
- 3   stalks celery, diced
- 6   russet potatoes, peeled and diced
- 2   cups frozen corn
- 1   can light coconut milk
- 2   tablespoons fresh parsley, chopped
-     Salt and pepper to taste

1. In a large pot, sauté the onion, garlic, carrots, and celery on medium-high heat in some of the low-sodium vegetable broth.

2. Once the vegetables soften, add the potatoes and remaining vegetable broth. Bring to a boil. If you need more liquid to bring the potatoes to a boil, add more broth or water.

3. Once the potatoes are softened, add frozen corn, coconut milk, fresh parsley, and salt and pepper to taste. Simmer for 45 minutes.

4. Enjoy in the best of health!

Plant to Plate
Creamy White Bean Soup

MAKES 6–8 SERVINGS

This creamy soup is a great recipe that helped me lose weight. It's so good that I eat this soup at least two times a month. White beans are loaded with fiber and protein, and combined with powerful kale and the amazing taste of rosemary, you'll soon find out why I love this soup so much!

- 1/2   cup low-sodium vegetable broth
- 1   onion, diced
- 3   carrots, diced
- 1   cup celery, finely diced
- 3   cloves garlic, minced
- 2   sprigs fresh rosemary, finely chopped
- 1   quart low-sodium vegetable broth
- 2   15-ounce BPA-free cans white beans, with liquid
- 4   cups curly kale
- 1   bay leaf
-     Kosher salt and pepper to taste

1. In stockpot over medium-high heat, sauté the onion, carrots, and celery in 1/2 cup of broth until softened.

2. Add the garlic and chopped rosemary and sauté for an additional 1–2 minutes.

3. Add the remaining low-sodium vegetable broth, the beans, and their liquid and bring to a boil. Reduce to a simmer and add the kale, bay leaf, salt, and pepper and cook for 30 minutes.

4. Remove the bay leaf from the soup and add soup to a high-powered blender. Puree until you get a creamy consistency.

5. Enjoy in the best of health!

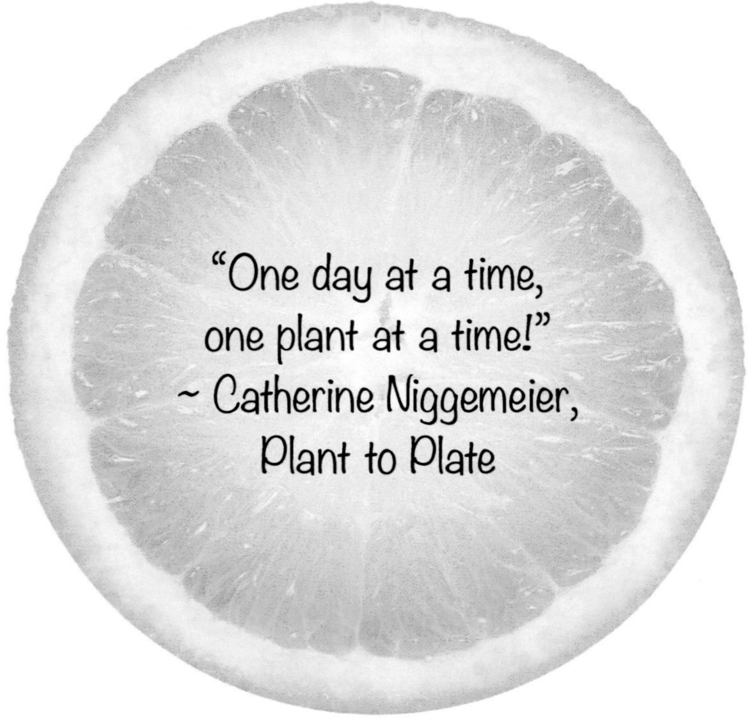

"One day at a time,
one plant at a time!"
~ Catherine Niggemeier,
Plant to Plate

Plant to Plate Minestrone

MAKES 6 SERVINGS

This ain't your mama's minestrone! Along with
pasta, I add potatoes for the nutritional benefits and
heartiness. This soup is loaded with flavor, fiber, and
beautiful color, and one of the things I love most
about plant-based eating is how appealing the food
is to the eye. Clients tell me that Plant to Plate food
looks so inviting, but I can't really take credit for it—
the vegetables show up and make everything look
great. And not only do they show up and look great,
they make everyone feel good.

1 large onion, diced
3 cloves garlic, minced
2 large carrots, diced
3 stalks celery, diced
1 cup low-sodium vegetable broth (for sautéing)
2 tablespoons tomato paste
2 teaspoons Italian seasoning
1 cup frozen cut green beans
1 cup of potatoes, diced
1 cup dried pasta
1 28-ounce can crushed tomatoes
2 cans cannellini beans, rinsed and drained
8 cups low-sodium vegetable broth
Salt and pepper to taste

1. In a large pot on medium-high heat, sauté
the onion, garlic, carrots, and celery in 1 cup of
vegetable broth.

2. Once the vegetables soften, add in Italian
seasoning and tomato paste. Cook for 2
minutes.

3. Add in green beans, potatoes, pasta,
tomatoes, cannellini beans, and remaining
vegetable broth. Bring to a boil, then lower the
heat and simmer for 40 minutes.

4. Season with salt and pepper to taste.

5. Enjoy in the best of health!

"When in doubt, eat a plant!"
~ Catherine Niggemeier,
Plant to Plate

Plant to Plate Black Bean Soup

MAKES 6 SERVINGS

Can you say FIBER? This heart-healthy soup is loaded with fiber and Mexican flavor. It has the perfect combination of flavors that wakes up your taste buds and gives your body so much love and goodness. This recipe is filled with vitamins and nutrients that nourish your health and will certainly please your palate.

1   16-ounce bag dried black beans
1   medium onion, chopped
4   cloves garlic, minced
1   red bell pepper, diced
1   green bell pepper, diced
3   cups low-sodium vegetable broth
3   teaspoons chili powder
2   teaspoons ground cumin
1   cup salsa
2   teaspoons lime juice
    Salt and pepper to taste

1. Rinse and sort black beans, looking for any stones or rocks that are sometimes found in dry beans. In a pot, cover with water and bring to a boil. Turn off the heat and let pot sit on the stove for an hour for beans to soften.

2. In a separate pot, sauté the onion, garlic, and red and green peppers in 1 cup of vegetable broth over medium-high heat until translucent, about 10 minutes.

3. Add chili powder and cumin and stir to combine.

4. Add beans, remaining vegetable broth, and salsa.

5. Bring to a boil, reduce to low heat, and simmer for 90 minutes. If needed, add more water to cover the beans. Do not let the beans dry out.

6. Remove from heat and stir in lime juice. Season with salt and pepper to taste.

7. Carefully transfer half of the mixture to a blender and puree until smooth. Mix puree back in with soup.

8. Enjoy in the best of health! 🩶

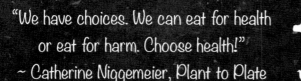

"We have choices. We can eat for health or eat for harm. Choose health!"
~ Catherine Niggemeier, Plant to Plate

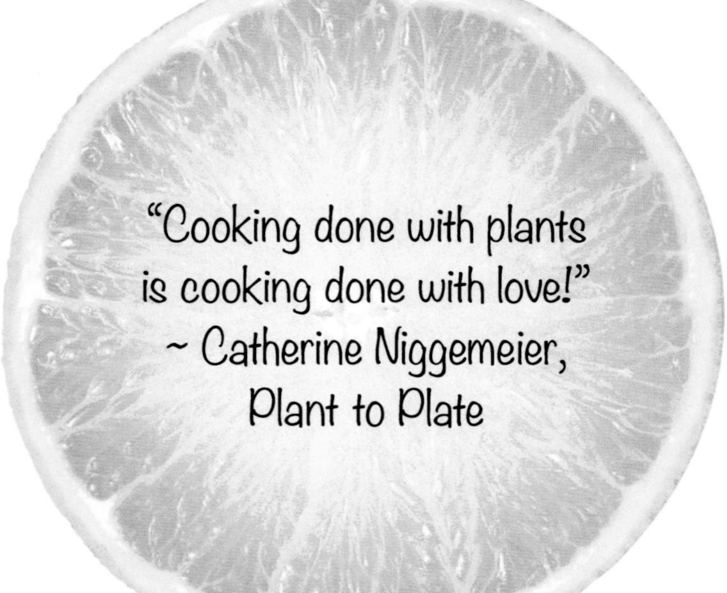

"Cooking done with plants
is cooking done with love!"
~ Catherine Niggemeier,
Plant to Plate

Plant to Plate Powerful Pea Soup

MAKES 2 QUARTS

The power of peas. This is one of my favorite soups, and I try to always have it on hand to enjoy. Peas are a powerhouse of antioxidants. They are anti-inflammatory, loaded with fiber to help control blood sugar, and help to protect your heart and digestive system. Dried peas have been around for centuries. This simple, powerful vegetable offers so much goodness for your body. Make use of it!

- 1 16-ounce bag dried green split peas, rinsed and sorted
- 1 large onion, diced
- 3 cloves garlic, minced
- 3 medium carrots, diced
- 2 stalks celery, diced
- 4 cups low-sodium vegetable broth
- 1 teaspoon Italian seasoning
- 3 yellow potatoes, diced
- 8 cups water
  Salt and pepper to taste

1. In a large strainer, rinse and sort the dried split peas. Set aside.

2. In a large pot on medium-high heat, sauté the onion, garlic, carrots, and celery in 1 cup vegetable broth.

3. Once the vegetables soften, add Italian seasoning and potatoes and sauté for additional 2 minutes.

4. Add the split peas, remaining vegetable broth, and water. Bring to a boil. Reduce heat to simmer. Season with salt and pepper to taste. Cover and cook for 90 minutes. If you like a smooth, creamy soup, place in blender and puree to desired consistency.

5. Enjoy in the best of health!

Plant to Plate Pea Soup with Tarragon

MAKES 6–8 SERVINGS

The perfect pairing of sweet peas and the unique taste of tarragon is so wonderful. My recipe is quick and loaded with wonderful nutrients that your body will thank you for.

- 2 medium leeks, washed well and finely chopped
- 1 clove garlic, minced
- 1/4 cup low-sodium vegetable broth for sautéing
- 3 cups water
- 4 cups thawed frozen peas
- 1 tablespoon fresh tarragon
  Salt and pepper to taste

1. In large pot, sauté leeks on medium-high heat in 1/4 cup low-sodium vegetable broth until softened, about 10 minutes.

2. Add garlic and sauté for another 2 minutes.

3. Add water and peas and cook for 20 minutes on medium-high heat. Remove from heat and let cool.

4. Add fresh tarragon.

5. Transfer to blender and puree soup until smooth and creamy. Season with salt and pepper to taste.

6. Enjoy in the best of health!

Plant to Plate Tennis Gazpacho

MAKES 4–6 SERVINGS

We call this Tennis Gazpacho because it is a family favorite of ours and was always requested by my girls after we played tennis on a hot Long Island summer day. We ate it so often that my girls now call this *Tennis Soup*! It's a refreshing, chilled soup that makes for a perfect lunch al fresco.

- 1 English cucumber with skin on, roughly chopped
- 1 red bell pepper, cored and seeded
- 1 orange bell pepper, cored and seeded
- 5 ripe plum tomatoes
- 1 large red onion
- 2 cloves garlic, minced
- 4 cups organic tomato juice
- 2 tablespoons red wine vinegar
  Salt and pepper to taste

1. Combine cucumbers, bell peppers, tomatoes, onion, and garlic in food processor. Pulse until roughly chopped.

2. In a large glass bowl, add the vegetable mixture, tomato juice, red wine vinegar, and salt and pepper. Mix well and chill.

3. Enjoy in the best of health!

Tip: The secret to the best-tasting Tennis Gazpacho is to let sit for 24 hours in the refrigerator prior to eating!

Plant to Plate Mexican Quinoa, pg. 80

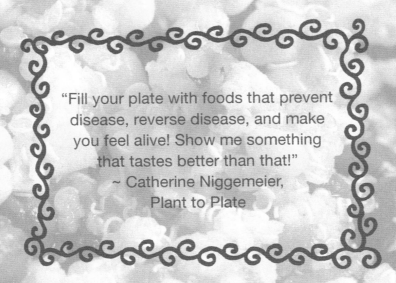

Sides and Salads

Although these recipes are called sides and salads, these dishes can often be used as full meals. The recipes are easy to make, loaded with healthy goodness, and so delicious. What I love most is that they are anti-inflammatory, which is a known fighter against diseases like cancer, type 2 diabetes, high blood pressure, high cholesterol, and heart disease. Best of all, they are so very easy to make!

"Fill your plate with foods that prevent disease, reverse disease, and make you feel alive! Show me something that tastes better than that!"
~ Catherine Niggemeier,
Plant to Plate

Plant to Plate Avocado Toast

Plant to Plate Elaine's Cool as a Cucumber Salad

Ava's Plant to Plate Avocado Toast

MAKES 2 SERVINGS

Why do I love this so much? Well, who doesn't love when someone you love makes you a meal? That's all it takes for me to love this recipe more and more each time Ava makes it for me.

- 1   ripe avocado
- 2   thick slices sourdough bread
- 1/2 cup cherry tomatoes, thinly sliced
- 2   tablespoons raw sunflower seeds
       Salt and pepper to taste

1. Cut and pit the avocado. Scoop out the flesh and mash.

2. Lightly toast the bread. Spread avocado evenly on bread. Top with sliced tomatoes, sprinkle the sunflower seeds, and season with salt and pepper to taste.

3. Enjoy in the best of health!

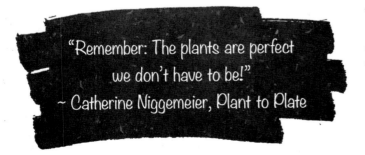

"Remember: The plants are perfect we don't have to be!"
~ Catherine Niggemeier, Plant to Plate

Plant to Plate Elaine's Cool as a Cucumber Salad

MAKES 4 SERVINGS

This recipe is inspired by a cucumber salad recipe by my mother-in-law, Elaine. I have just added a little twist to it. I love this salad on top of anything or as a stand-alone dish. It lasts several days in the refrigerator—or maybe not. It's a family favorite and gone before you know it!

For the best results, make this with a mandolin to get paper-thin cucumber and onion slices. If you don't have a mandolin, slice the cucumbers and onion as thin as possible.

- 2   large English cucumbers, thinly sliced
- 1   large white onion, thinly sliced
- 1   cup fresh dill, chopped
- 1   teaspoon salt
- 1/2 cup white vinegar
- 1   teaspoon white sugar
       Salt and pepper to taste

1. In a large bowl, add cucumbers, onion, dill, and 1 teaspoon salt.

2. Cover and chill in refrigerator for 1 hour to draw out the flavor.

3. Remove from refrigerator and add white vinegar and sugar.

4. Toss and season with salt and pepper to taste. Chill for 30 minutes and serve.

5. Enjoy in the best of health!

Plant to Plate Happy Sunflower Salad

Plant to Plate
"B"LT Sandwich

MAKES 2 OPEN-FACED SANDWICHES

This isn't what you are thinking, because it is way better for your health and your heart. The "B" in this recipe stands for BEANS!

2	hearty slices sourdough bread
1/2	cup Hannah's Plant to Plate Hummus (pg. 48)
4	slices beefsteak tomato
2	Bibb lettuce leaves
1	ripe avocado, peeled, pitted, and sliced

1. Lightly toast sourdough bread.

2. Spread hummus evenly on each slice of bread, top with sliced avocado, 2 slices of tomato, and 1 Bibb lettuce leaf.

3. Enjoy in the best of health!

> "Don't make it complicated. Focus on wanting better health for yourself at every meal and good health will follow!"
> ~ Catherine Niggemeier, Plant to Plate

Plant to Plate
Happy Sunflower Salad

MAKES 4 SERVINGS

Enjoy this served on romaine leaves, red cabbage leaves, collard greens, or your favorite bread. It is a family favorite and one that I featured on television here in New York.

2	cups sunflower seeds
1/2	cup water
3	tablespoons red wine vinegar
1	teaspoon salt
2	cups celery, finely diced
1-1/2	cups red pepper, finely diced
1/2	cup cherry tomatoes, diced
1/2	cup scallions, finely diced

1. Soak the sunflower seeds for at least 3 hours, then drain.

2. In a food processor, blend sunflower seeds and water to a fine paste.

3. Add red wine vinegar and salt, then pulse again. Transfer to a large bowl.

4. Fold in celery, red pepper, tomatoes, and scallions.

5. Enjoy in the best of health!

Plant to Plate Mexican Quinoa

MAKES 4 SERVINGS

Quinoa is a nutrient-dense powerhouse that is a great option for something different from your typical recipe of rice and beans. It is loaded with fiber, protein, and all the essential amino acids your body needs.

- 3 cloves garlic, minced
- 1 cup quinoa
- 1 cup low-sodium vegetable broth
- 1 can black beans, drained and rinsed
- 1 can fire-roasted diced tomatoes
- 1 cup frozen corn
- 1 teaspoon chili powder
- 1 teaspoon cumin
- 3 tablespoons Italian parsley, chopped
  Juice of 1 lime
  Salt and pepper to taste
- 1 ripe avocado, cubed

1. Sauté the garlic in a bit of the vegetable broth for 1–2 minutes.

2. Add quinoa, remaining vegetable broth, beans, tomatoes, corn, chili powder, and cumin. Bring to a boil. Cover, reduce heat, and simmer for about 20 minutes until quinoa is cooked.

3. Stir in lime juice and parsley.

4. Season with salt and pepper to taste. Serve with fresh avocado on top.

5. Enjoy in the best of health!

Plant to Plate Lentil and Butternut Squash Salad

MAKES 6 SERVINGS

Don't think salads are over when fall arrives. It's the perfect time to use butternut squash for this delicious salad. French lentils are one of the greatest gifts Mother Nature gives us. They are a nutrient-dense food packed with protein and fiber and are so versatile. Enjoy this dish any time of day, including as a get-up-and-go breakfast.

- 1/2 cup walnuts
- 2 cups butternut squash, coarsely diced
- 2 tablespoons low-sodium vegetable broth
  Kosher salt and pepper to taste
- 1 cup French lentils, cooked and cooled
- 2 cups parsley leaves, torn
  Plant to Plate Vinaigrette (pg. 57)
- 1 apple, thinly sliced

1. Preheat oven to 375 degrees. On a baking sheet, add the walnuts, making an even layer. Toast until golden, about 10–12 minutes. Cool slightly, then roughly chop.

2. Turn oven up to 425 degrees. On another baking sheet, add the squash and spread in an even layer. Toss with low-sodium vegetable broth and season with kosher salt and freshly ground black pepper. Roast until the squash is golden brown and tender, about 20–25 minutes.

3. In a large bowl, add the lentils, squash, half of the walnuts, and 1/4 cup vinaigrette. Toss to combine, then add the parsley and season with kosher salt and freshly ground black pepper.

4. Garnish with apples and remaining walnuts.

5. Enjoy in the best of health!

Plant to Plate Lentil and
Butternut Squash Salad

Plant to Plate Mexican Quinoa

Plant to Plate
Broccoli Love Salad

MAKES 6–8 SERVINGS

This salad is a huge hit in the Plant to Plate kitchen and the one I hear about the most when clients tell me what they add to their weekly repertoires when they want to increase their plant-based meals and fiber.

- 6 cups small broccoli florets, blanched
- 2 cups carrots, shredded
- 1 cup walnuts, chopped
  Plant to Plate Love Dressing (pg. 57)
  Salt and pepper to taste

1. Place all ingredients in a large bowl and toss well.

2. Drizzle with Plant to Plate Love Dressing and serve.

3. Enjoy in the best of health!

Cooking tip: It is important to blanch the broccoli. Blanching brings out a gorgeous color in the broccoli and makes this dish pop with color. It also takes away that bitterness that raw broccoli can sometimes have. This method cooks the broccoli slightly but leaves the broccoli crisp and fresh.

How to blanch broccoli: Bring a large pot of water to a full boil. Add the broccoli florets and boil for 90 seconds. Remove florets with a slotted spoon and immediately place in an ice water bath to stop the cooking process. Remove from ice water and continue with recipe.

Plant to Plate
Orzo Salad

MAKES 6–8 SERVINGS

A summertime favorite around the Plant to Plate kitchen! This is a great dish to have on hand in the refrigerator to accompany grilled vegetables. Think fresh tomatoes and basil and eating al fresco in the summertime sun.

- 1 pound orzo
- 3/4 cup red onion, chopped
- 1/2 cup fresh basil, chopped
- 1/2 cup fresh cherry tomatoes
- 1 can garbanzo beans, drained and rinsed
  Plant to Plate Red Wine Vinaigrette (pg. 57)
  Salt and pepper to taste

1. Cook orzo according to package instructions. Drain and set aside to cool in a large bowl.

2. Toss in the chopped onion and basil, cherry tomatoes, and garbanzo beans.

3. Slowly add red wine vinaigrette until salad is dressed to your liking. Season with salt and pepper to taste.

4. Serve at room temperature or chill in the fridge.

5. Enjoy in the best of health!

"Think plant thoughts!"
~ Catherine Niggemeier, Plant to Plate

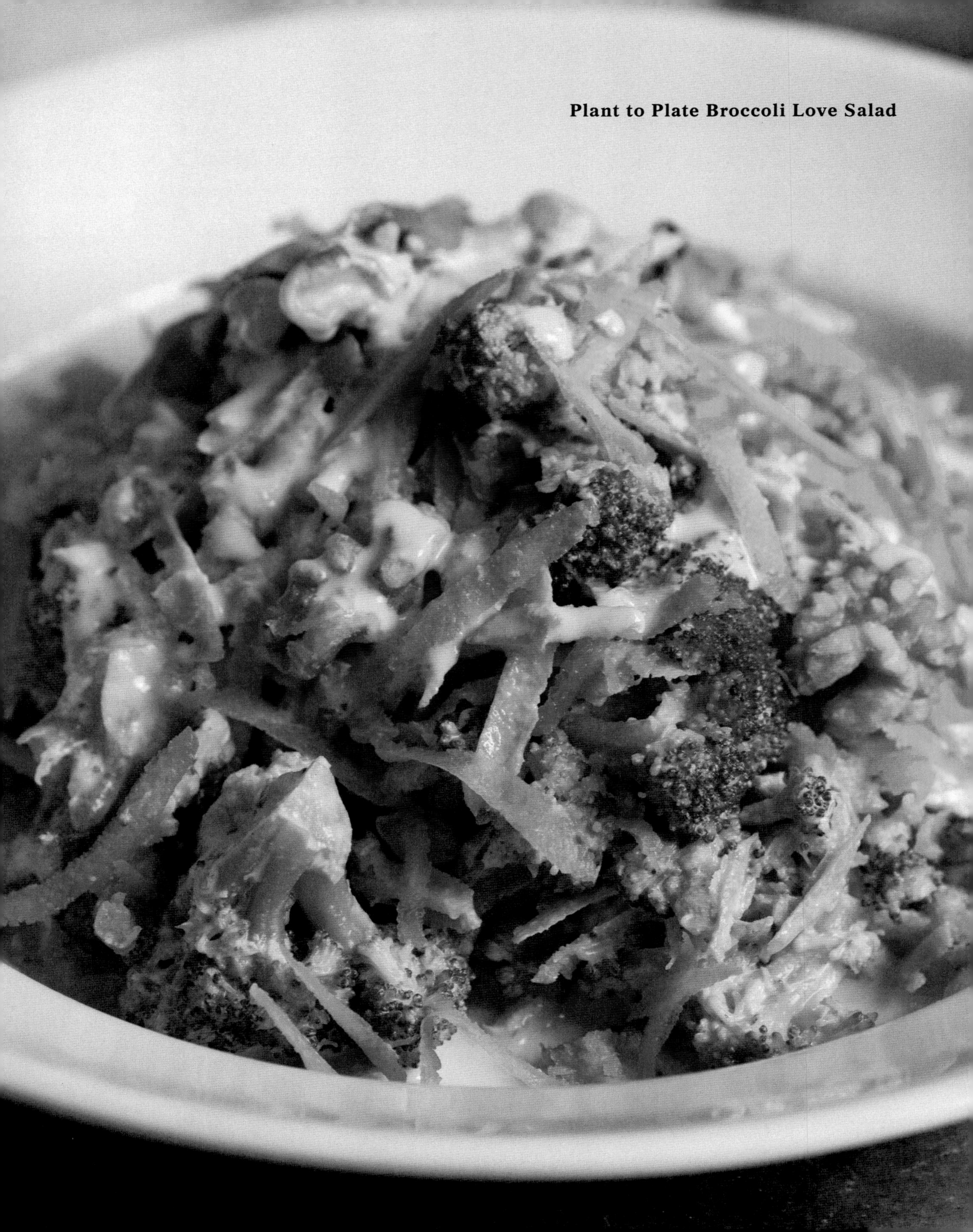
Plant to Plate Broccoli Love Salad

Plant to Plate
Thankful Salad

MAKES 1–2 SERVINGS

Every time I eat this salad, I am so thankful for what it does for my health. It's so yummy and filling that it became the go-to salad of my Plant to Plate cooking classes. There wasn't a single client who didn't love it. The warmth of the vegetables and the toasted nuts make a hearty meal.

For this recipe, you can roast any vegetable that you enjoy! Roasting vegetable times vary.

1	sweet potato, cubed
1/2	butternut squash, cubed
	Juice of 1 lemon
1/2	cup nuts, such as walnuts or almonds
	Salad greens

1. Preheat oven to 425 degrees. Line baking sheet with unbleached parchment paper.

2. Toast nuts in a dry pan on medium-high heat for 5 minutes.

3. Toss cubed sweet potato and butternut squash in the lemon juice. Place in oven to roast for 30–35 minutes.

4. Plate the salad greens, top with roasted vegetables, and add the toasted nuts. Drizzle lightly with your favorite Plant to Plate dressing or fresh lemon.

5. Enjoy in the best of health! 🩶

"Come join me in the 13%!"
~ Catherine Niggemeier, Plant to Plate

Plant to Plate
Black Bean Avocado Salad

MAKES 4–6 SERVINGS

If this dish doesn't make you think of summertime, I don't know what will. I strongly recommend that you roast the corn for this recipe, as it adds an incredible flavor to the dish. Serve al fresco in the garden as a meal or pair it beautifully with other dishes on your summertime table.

1	cup roasted corn kernels
2	cups cherry tomatoes, halved
1	orange bell pepper, seeded and diced
1	can black beans, rinsed and drained
1/3	cup red onion, diced
	Juice of 2 limes
2	ripe avocados, coarsely diced
	Salt and pepper to taste

1. On a very hot grill, place washed corn on the cob (leave the corn slightly wet for roasting) and grill until corn is fully roasted. If you don't have time to grill the corn, you can use frozen corn as a substitute.

2. Place tomatoes, bell pepper, black beans, onion, and corn in a large bowl.

3. Pour the lime juice over the other ingredients and toss well.

4. Fold in diced avocado and season with salt and pepper to taste. Served chilled or at room temperature.

5. Enjoy in the best of health!

Plant to Plate Beet and Walnut Salad

MAKES 4 SERVINGS

This recipe calls for one of my favorite easy to-go packaged foods—precooked beets! Precooked beets are so convenient to have on hand. My girls take them to school for lunch. We also love them on salads and enjoy them on top of toast with some raw onion. This dish is always a crowd-pleaser, even for those people who think they don't like beets.

12	precooked beets
1/2	cup chopped walnuts
2	tablespoons Dijon mustard
2	tablespoons red wine vinegar
1	minced shallot
2	tablespoons fresh lemon juice
1/2	teaspoon white sugar

1. Toast walnuts in a dry pan for 5 minutes to bring out the flavor.

2. In a bowl, whisk together the mustard, vinegar, shallots, lemon juice, and white sugar.

3. Cut beets into 1-inch pieces. Add to a large bowl and drizzle with the desired amount of dressing. Top with toasted walnuts and season with salt and pepper to taste.

4. Chill for 30 minutes and serve.

5. Enjoy in the best of health! 🩶

Hannah's Plant to Plate Pico de Gallo Cucumber Boats

MAKES 8 SERVINGS

I love to see my daughters getting creative in the kitchen. My Hannah created this dish for us one summer's night after she picked some fresh tomatoes and cilantro from our garden. A few simple ingredients and some flavorful spices made for a hearty, delicious dish.

1	can chickpeas, rinsed and drained
1	teaspoon cumin
3	cups ripe tomatoes, diced (about 3–4 medium tomatoes)
1	cup red onion, finely chopped
1	cup fresh cilantro, chopped
1	lime, zested and juiced
1	teaspoon white sugar
	Salt and pepper to taste

For the boats:

2	large English cucumbers, seeded and cut lengthwise into quarters

1. In a large bowl, combine all ingredients.

2. Mix well and chill for one hour.

3. Serve over the cucumber boats.

4. Enjoy in the best of health!

> "Keep calm and cook plants!"
> ~ Catherine Niggemeier, Plant to Plate

Plant to Plate Beet and Walnut Salad

"Always cook with your heart
and for your heart!"
~ Catherine Niggemeier,
Plant to Plate

Plant to Plate
Coconut Carrot Rice

MAKES 8 SERVINGS

This is a great dish for all seasons, and it always has a place at my Thanksgiving table. Simple, fast, and nutritious, it is always enjoyed by all.

- 1/2 cup low-sodium vegetable broth
- 1 medium onion, diced
- 2 tablespoons garlic, minced
- 1 tablespoon curry powder
- 1 15-ounce can pinto beans, drained and rinsed
- 4 cups water
- 1 13.5-ounce can unsweetened light coconut milk
- 2 cups carrots, diced
- 2 cups uncooked brown rice
- 2 cups fresh spinach
  Salt and pepper to taste

1. In a large pot on medium-high heat, sauté the onion and garlic in vegetable broth until soft.

2. Add curry powder and pinto beans and mix together. Add water, coconut milk, carrots, and rice. Bring to a boil, then reduce heat to low. Cover and cook for 35 minutes.

3. In the last 5 minutes, add in spinach. Season with salt and pepper and serve.

4. Enjoy in the best of health!

Plant to Plate
Who Stole the Cheese?

MAKES 1 CUP

Yes! I said cheese! This is a great cheese that you can add to so many dishes, free of milk proteins that can be harmful to our health. I love when clients try this dish because they can't believe it is made from cashews. It adds a great layer of flavor to potatoes or your favorite cooked vegetables.

- 1 cup raw cashews
- 4 tablespoons nutritional yeast
- 1 teaspoon sea salt
- 1/2 teaspoon garlic powder
- 1/4 teaspoon Italian seasoning

1. In a food processor, place all ingredients and mix/pulse into a fine meal.

2. Enjoy in the best of health!

"Give your babies healthy habits
and they will grow up
to be healthy adults!"
~ Catherine Niggemeier,
Plant to Plate

What's for Dinner?

No matter if you live by yourself, with a significant other, or have a large family of kids, this is usually the big question at the end of the day. The answer is always the same in my house—PLANTS!

This section contains simple, quick recipes, and if you have beans in your pantry and some fresh or frozen produce, you have already fought half the battle of weeknight dinners.

All of the recipes in this book have been tested on more than a thousand people and they have all received rave reviews.

Steve's Plant to Plate Bean Burgers

Steve's Plant to Plate Bean Burgers

MAKES 6 PATTIES

Yes! Burgers. I started living a whole-food, plant-based lifestyle in April 2014, and within three days, I quickly realized that that I had never felt this great before in my life. I love this burger for so many reasons. First, Steve created it. Second, I love the taste and texture. As a bonus, it is cruelty-free, environmentally friendly, and so good for me! I hope you try it and add it to your repertoire!

2	cans black beans, rinsed and drained
2	tablespoons garlic powder
1	tablespoon Italian seasoning
1	teaspoon onion powder
1/4	cup ketchup
2	tablespoons Dijon mustard
1	teaspoon salt
1/2	teaspoon ground pepper
1	cup cooked short-grain brown rice
1	cup rolled oats
1/2	cup chickpea flour

1. Preheat oven to 375 degrees. Line baking sheet with unbleached parchment paper.

2. In a food processor, blend together the black beans, garlic powder, Italian seasoning, onion powder, ketchup, mustard, pepper, and salt.

3. Transfer mixture to a large mixing bowl. Fold in rolled oats and cooked brown rice.

4. Form patties and dredge in chickpea flour (this gives it a nice crispy texture!).

5. Place the patties on the baking sheet and bake for 20–25 minutes, or until browned.

6. Serve on your favorite bun with lettuce, fresh tomato, and avocado.

7. Enjoy in the best of health!

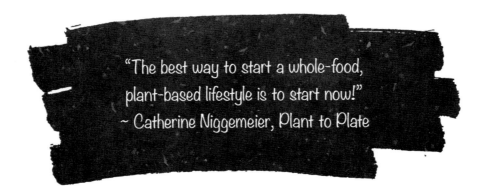

"The best way to start a whole-food, plant-based lifestyle is to start now!"
~ Catherine Niggemeier, Plant to Plate

Plant to Plate
Layers of Love Lasagna

MAKES 6–8 SERVINGS

This lasagna was created by my mom, Rosemary McMenamin, who has always shown me many layers of love. During Christmas of 2014, my mom wanted to make me something plant-based that I could enjoy as my meal. Growing up in her house, I remember her always trying new dishes, so I was not surprised she created something special for me, once again showing me love.

It was the best lasagna I'd ever had in my life, and I have since made this many times for my Plant to Plate classes and as a great dinner for my family!

2	cups raw cashews
12	lasagna noodles
1	15-ounce can pumpkin
1	clove garlic
1/8	teaspoon Italian seasoning
1	teaspoon salt
	Water for blending
3	tablespoons low-sodium vegetable broth
2	cloves garlic, minced
8	ounces mushrooms, sliced
8	ounces Brussels sprouts, shredded
6	cups kale, stemmed and chopped
5	cups Plant to Plate Healthy Heart Tomato Sauce (pg. 53)

> "You only live once.
> Eat plants and live it well!"
> ~ Catherine Niggemeier, Plant to Plate

1. Preheat oven to 350 degrees. Soak cashews in water for 30 minutes.

2. Cook lasagna noodles according to package instructions. Drain and rinse with cold water. Drain again and set aside to dry.

3. Drain soaked cashews. Place soaked cashews in a blender or food processor. Blend, adding about 1/8 cup water (more if needed) to smooth out the cashews.

4. Add pumpkin, 1 clove garlic, Italian seasoning, and salt to the blender. Cover and process until nearly smooth. You want the mixture to have a Ricotta cheese consistency.

5. In a large skillet, heat vegetable broth over medium heat. Add minced garlic and cook and stir for 30 seconds or until fragrant. Do not let garlic burn.

6. Add mushrooms and Brussels sprouts and cook for 5–7 minutes or until tender. Gradually add kale, tossing and cooking for 2–3 minutes or until wilted. Remove from heat.

7. Assemble lasagna, first spreading 1 cup tomato sauce on the bottom of a 3-quart rectangular baking dish. Next layer with 3 lasagna noodles, one-third of the "cheese" mixture, and one-third of the vegetable mixture. Reserve some of the vegetables for topping. Repeat layers twice. Top with remaining lasagna noodles and remaining sauce.

8. Cover loosely with foil and bake for 45 minutes. Uncover and bake for 10–15 minutes or until heated through. Add small amount of sautéed shredded Brussels sprouts for top garnish.

9. Enjoy in the best of health!

Plant to Plate Falfel

Plant to Plate
Falafel

MAKES 6 LARGE FALAFEL

I love to have these on hand in my refrigerator. They're so easy and convenient for a quick meal. You can quickly heat up falafel and make yourself a hearty sandwich with all the trimmings of fresh onion, tomato, and lettuce. Serve this with Plant to Plate Tahini Sauce (pg. 53).

- 2 cloves garlic
- 1/2 cup Italian parsley
- 1/2 cup scallions, chopped
- 2 cans chickpeas, rinsed and drained
- 1 cup rolled oats
- 2-1/2 tablespoons fresh lemon juice
- 2 teaspoons ground cumin
- 1 teaspoon ground turmeric
- 1-1/2 teaspoons ground coriander
- 1 teaspoon salt
- 1/4 teaspoon pepper

1. Preheat oven to 375 degrees. Line a baking sheet with unbleached parchment paper.

2. Place garlic, parsley, and scallions in the food processor and process until mixture is finely chopped.

3. Add all other ingredients and process until ingredients are blended. You want the mixture to hold together firmly. Refrigerate for 30 minutes.

4. Form into patties.

5. Place the patties on the baking sheet and bake for 20–25 minutes, or until browned.

6. Enjoy in the best of health!

Plant to Plate
No-Cheese Quesadillas

MAKES 4–8 SERVINGS

Prep all of the quesadillas first. The pan will get hotter as you go, so cooking will go faster with each one you make!

- 8 10-inch flour tortillas
- 1/2 cup chopped scallions
- 1/2 to 1 cup salsa
- 3 tablespoons Hannah's Plant to Plate Hummus (pg. 48)

1. Heat a large skillet on medium-high heat and place your tortilla in the middle.

2. Spread 3 heaping tablespoons of Hannah's Plant to Plate hummus on a tortilla, sprinkle some chopped scallions, and add a thin layer of salsa. Top with second tortilla and add to skillet, cooking until golden on each side, approximately 3–5 minutes.

3. Cut each quesadilla into 8 triangles and serve with more hummus.

4. Enjoy in the best of health!

"Love yourself enough to give yourself the gift and benefits of plants!"
~ Catherine Niggemeier, Plant to Plate

Plant to Plate Lentil Meatballs

MAKES 12 MEATBALLS

These taste wonderful paired with Plant to Plate Healthy Heart Tomato Sauce (pg. 53), on pasta, or on sub rolls, which is how my family likes to eat them! There is no sacrifice for flavor in these delicious lentil meatballs.

2	tablespoons ground flax seed
2-1/2	tablespoons warm water
2	cups green lentils, rinsed and drained
4	cups water
1/2	red onion, minced
1/2	cup low-sodium vegetable broth
1	large carrot, grated
2	stalks celery, finely chopped
3	cloves garlic, minced
1/2	cup rolled oats
2	tablespoons fresh parsley, chopped
1	cup seasoned Italian breadcrumbs
1	teaspoon paprika
1	teaspoon garlic powder
1	teaspoon Italian seasoning
	Salt and pepper to taste

1. Preheat oven to 375 degrees. Line a baking sheet with unbleached parchment paper.

2. Combine the flax seed and 2 1/2 tablespoons warm water in a small bowl. Mix and let stand for 10 minutes until it becomes a gel. This is your binder.

3. Bring 4 cups of water to a boil. Add the lentils and a pinch of salt and return to a boil. Lower the heat, cover, and cook for about 20 minutes, until the water is absorbed.

4. Remove from heat and let cool, then transfer the lentils to a food processor. Process lentils until smooth.

5. Heat a large skillet on medium-high heat. Add the onion and sauté them in low-sodium vegetable broth until translucent, about 4 minutes. Add the grated carrot, celery, garlic, salt, and pepper. Sauté about 5 minutes until the veggies are tender. Set aside to cool.

6. Add the rolled oats, veggies, parsley, spices, and flax gel to the lentils in the food processor and process until smooth. Transfer the mixture to a large bowl.

7. Add the breadcrumbs, 1/4 cup at a time, to the lentil mixture and stir until well mixed. Add breadcrumbs until you reach your desired consistency. Mixture should be firm and hold up as a meatball. If it feels too moist, slowly add more breadcrumbs. You may not need the entire cup.

8. Put the lentil mixture into the fridge for about 30 minutes. Once chilled, use a spoon to scoop the lentil mixture and then use your hands to roll it into a golf-ball-sized meatball. Roll it until it feels sturdy.

9. Place lentil meatballs on baking sheet and bake for 15 minutes, then roll the meatballs to the other side. Continue baking for another 15 minutes.

10. Set aside and serve with Plant to Plate Healthy Heart Tomato Sauce (pg. 53).

11. Enjoy in the best of health!

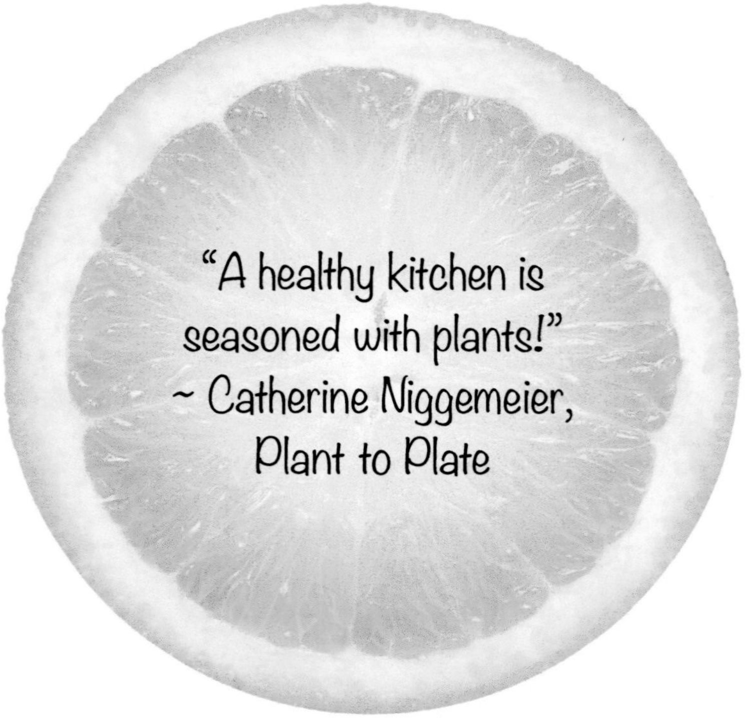

"A healthy kitchen is
seasoned with plants!"
~ Catherine Niggemeier,
Plant to Plate

Plant to Plate
Pasta Fagioli

MAKES 8 SERVINGS

This dish is great to enjoy during the fall and winter months for Sunday dinner. It pairs well with Plant to Plate Thankful Salad (pg. 84) and a hearty sourdough bread. This is a quick dinner to make, and if there are any leftovers, it's perfect for a school lunch on Monday.

While you can use regular crushed tomatoes, trust me when I say that there's no comparison when it comes to San Marzano tomatoes!

5	cups low-sodium vegetable broth
1	sweet onion, diced
3	stalks celery, diced
3	carrots, diced
4	cloves garlic, minced
1/4	cup tomato paste
2	teaspoons Italian seasoning
2	cans cannellini beans, rinsed and drained
1	28-ounce can San Marzano whole tomatoes
1	cup uncooked ditalini pasta or other small pasta
5	basil leaves, stemmed and chopped
	Salt and pepper to taste

1. In a bowl, use your hands to break up the tomatoes into smaller chunks. Save the juice!

2. In a pot, sauté the onion, celery, carrots, and garlic in about half a cup of vegetable broth until translucent.

3. Add in tomato paste and Italian seasoning and stir together for a minute.

4. Add in beans, San Marzano tomatoes, and remaining vegetable broth. Add more liquid if desired. Cook for 30 minutes.

5. Add in pasta and cook for another 8 minutes. At the end, add in basil and salt and pepper to taste.

6. Enjoy in the best of health!

Plant to Plate
UnBEETable Burger

MAKES 4 BURGERS

Go ahead, I dare you to say that you don't enjoy this burger! I love the look on people's faces when they come to the Plant to Plate kitchen and hear that we are making beet burgers because most are not impressed by the sound of it. But the best is by the end of class, they'll have completely changed their minds and are asking for seconds! Beets are amazing, and the flavor can't be "beet."

1-1/2	cups cooked brown rice
1	cup precooked beets, chopped
1	cup cooked French lentils
1/2	teaspoon salt
	Pepper to taste
1	teaspoon Italian seasoning
1	teaspoon mustard
3	tablespoons onion, finely chopped
2	cloves garlic, minced
1/2	cup rolled oats

1. Preheat oven to 375 degrees. Line baking sheet with unbleached parchment paper.

2. In a food processor, pulse the rice and add in chopped beets until the mixture comes together but still has texture.

3. Pour into bowl and add remaining ingredients and mix well. Form into patties.

4. Place the patties on the baking sheet and bake for 20–25 minutes.

5. Enjoy in the best of health!

"Good health starts in your gut.
Feed it plants because it's
hungry for nutrients!"
~ Catherine Niggemeier,
Plant to Plate

Plant to Plate Stromboli

MAKES 8 SERVINGS

Everyone loves when it's Stromboli time in the Plant to Plate kitchen! This is a favorite from my Italian plant-based cooking class and a great dish to bring to a Super Bowl party to share with football fans. Even your biggest meat eaters will enjoy this dish!

1	cup yellow onion, sliced
1/2	cup low-sodium vegetable broth
1	cup red bell peppers, thinly sliced
1	cup green bell peppers, thinly sliced
2	tablespoons garlic, minced
1	teaspoon Italian seasoning
	Store-bought pizza dough
	Plant to Plate Pesto (pg. 50)

1. Preheat oven to 375 degrees. Line baking sheet with unbleached parchment paper.

2. In a large skillet, sauté the onion in vegetable broth. Add the bell peppers and cook, stirring occasionally, until very soft, about 4–5 minutes.

3. Add the garlic and Italian seasoning and cook, stirring, for 1 minute. Remove from heat and let cool.

4. On a lightly floured surface, roll the dough into a large rectangle, about 10 × 14 inches. Spread the pesto sauce evenly over the dough, leaving a 1-inch border all around.

5. Spoon the sautéed vegetables on top of the pesto sauce, then roll the dough in a Swiss-roll fashion. Start at one end and keep rolling and tucking in until the entire dough is used. Twist the ends to seal both sides. Gently slice 2 cuts into the top to allow steam to escape while cooking.

6. Bake until golden brown and starting to crisp, about 30 minutes.

7. Enjoy in the best of health!

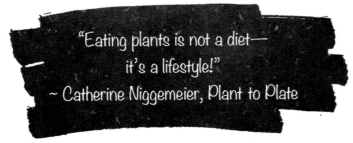

"Eating plants is not a diet— it's a lifestyle!"
~ Catherine Niggemeier, Plant to Plate

Plant to Plate
Chili

MAKES 8 SERVINGS

This is a big crowd-pleaser to serve to a group after a cold day outside or perfect to make for batch cooking to bring along all week in your favorite lunch thermos.

1/2	cup low-sodium vegetable broth
1	large onion, diced
1	cup carrots, shredded
1	red pepper, diced
1	yellow pepper, diced
1	jalapeno pepper, cleaned and minced
4	cloves garlic, minced
2	tablespoons chili powder
2	tablespoons cumin
1	teaspoon dried oregano
1	28-ounce can crushed tomatoes
2	15-ounce cans kidney beans, drained and rinsed
1	can black beans, drained and rinsed
	Salt and pepper to taste

1. In a large pot, sauté the onion, shredded carrots, red pepper, yellow pepper, and jalapeno pepper in vegetable broth until softened.

2. Add in the garlic and sauté for 1 minute.

3. Add in chili powder, cumin, and oregano and sauté for another minute.

4. Add tomatoes and beans. Bring to a boil and simmer for 40 minutes on low heat. Season with salt and pepper to taste.

5. Enjoy in the best of health!

Plant to Plate
Spaghetti Carbonara

MAKES 6–8 SERVINGS

This ain't your momma's carbonara! It's loaded with health and yumminess without all the saturated fat and calories of traditional carbonara. If I served you this and didn't tell you it was plant-based, you would have no idea!

2	carrots
1/2	onion
1	medium yellow zucchini, finely diced
1	medium green zucchini, finely diced
1	teaspoon garlic powder
3	tablespoons nutritional yeast
2	teaspoons cornstarch
1/3	cup plant-based milk (pg. 41)
1	pound cooked spaghetti noodles
	Salt and pepper to taste

1. Boil carrots and onion until soft. Drain and set aside.

2. Heat low-sodium vegetable broth in a large skillet on medium-high heat. Brown the zucchini until tender.

3. In a blender, combine cooked carrots and onion, garlic powder, nutritional yeast, cornstarch, and milk. Blend until smooth.

4. Pour mixture over zucchini, mix well, and pour over spaghetti noodles. Season with salt and pepper to taste.

5. Enjoy in the best of health!

"Wake up today and eat more plants!"
~ Catherine Niggemeier,
Plant to Plate

Plant to Plate Soft Tacos

MAKES 4 TACOS

This is a family favorite! You can let your plant-based imagination and creativity run wild and use whatever plants your family enjoys! Believe me when I tell you that sweet potatoes are the best swap for traditional tacos served with ground meat. Nothing compares to the health benefits that sweet potatoes give you!

2–3	sweet potatoes
1/4	cup low-sodium vegetable broth
1/2	teaspoon salt
1/4	teaspoon pepper
1	small yellow onion, diced
2	cloves garlic, minced
1	teaspoon cumin
2	teaspoons chili powder
4	tortillas
1	can black beans, rinsed and drained

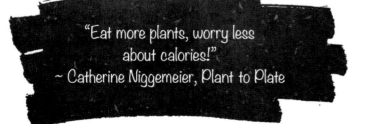

"Eat more plants, worry less about calories!"
~ Catherine Niggemeier, Plant to Plate

1. Preheat oven to 425 degrees.

2. Peel and dice sweet potatoes into 1/2-inch cubes. Toss in low-sodium vegetable broth, reserving 1–2 tablespoons for later, and sprinkle with salt and pepper. Line a baking sheet with parchment paper, spread the potatoes out in an even layer, and roast for 30 minutes, turning once.

3. Heat a skillet on medium-high heat and sauté the onion for 10 minutes in remaining low-sodium vegetable broth.

4. Add in garlic and sauté for 2 minutes. Add black beans, cumin, and chili powder. Season with salt and pepper. Continue cooking on medium heat for 20 minutes. You may need to add a few tablespoons of water to prevent the pan from getting too dry.

5. In your still-warm oven, heat the tortillas for 2 minutes.

6. Now the fun the begins! Place tortilla on a dinner plate and layer the roasted sweet potatoes as your base, add the black beans mixture, then top with your favorites. We love sliced avocado with organic salsa. If you want, you can leave out the tortilla and serve over rice.

7. Enjoy in the best of health! 🤍

"Be kind to yourself,
you deserve it!"
~ Catherine Niggemeier,
Plant to Plate

Plant to Plate Who Stole the Cheese Au Gratin

MAKES 4–6 SERVINGS

Think cheesy, creamy casserole in this amazing dish of health. Who says living a whole-food, plant-based lifestyle has to be boring and free of indulgences? Go ahead and make this for your family and friends, and then tell them afterwards how you made this dish without cheese. I am sure they won't believe you!

2	pints Brussels sprouts, trimmed and halved
2	large yellow onions, thinly sliced
1	large bunch of asparagus, cut into 2-inch pieces
1/4	cup low-sodium vegetable broth
2	tablespoons low-sodium vegetable broth
1	teaspoon salt
	Pinch of black pepper
1	cup Plant to Plate Who Stole the Cheese? (pg. 89)

1. Preheat oven to 425 degrees.

2. In a 12-inch cast-iron skillet, sauté onion in 1/4 cup of low-sodium vegetable broth on medium heat until softened, being careful not to burn it. Add more broth if needed for sautéing.

3. In a large bowl, toss Brussels sprouts and asparagus together, then add 2 tablespoons of low-sodium vegetable broth and mix well to get the vegetables coated.

4. Add salt, black pepper, and half of the Plant to Plate Who Stole the Cheese mixture, coating vegetables well.

5. Spread the slightly cooled onions around in the bottom of the skillet to create an even base. Top with Brussels sprouts and asparagus mixture.

6. Top with an even layer of the remaining Plant to Plate Who Stole the Cheese mixture and bake at 425 degrees for 25–30 minutes.

7. Rest before serving.

8. Enjoy in the best of health!

"It is up to you to focus on true health!"
~ Catherine Niggemeier, Plant to Plate

Plant to Plate Mushroom Stroganoff

Plant to Plate Mushroom Stroganoff

MAKES 4–6 SERVINGS

This is a favorite hearty dish that I make throughout our cold winter months here in New York. It is best served over rice. The best thing about this stroganoff is how healthy it is for you. The creamy taste and amazing texture will bring the best plant-based smile to your face!

- 3/4 cup raw cashews
- 1/3 cup water
- 1 tablespoon red wine vinegar
- 1/2 sweet onion, diced
- 2 pounds white mushrooms, sliced
- 3 tablespoons Dijon mustard
- 1 cup low-sodium vegetable broth
  Salt and pepper to taste

1. Soak the cashews in a bowl of water for an hour.

2. Drain and place cashews in blender. Add in 1/3 cup water, vinegar, and a pinch of salt. Blend until you get a smooth and creamy consistency.

3. Heat a cast-iron skillet on medium-high heat and sauté the onion and mushrooms in 1/4 cup low-sodium vegetable broth. Make sure you have enough liquid while sautéing that you do not burn the skillet. Stir frequently until the mushrooms are browned, about 10 minutes.

4. Add in remaining broth and mustard and bring to a boil. Lower the heat and simmer until the mushrooms become softened, then stir in the cashew cream. Season with salt and pepper to taste.

5. Serve over prepared rice.

6. Enjoy in the best of health!

Plant to Plate No Cheese, Please Potato Au Gratin

MAKES 4–6 SERVINGS

You say po-tay-to, I say po-tah-to. However you say it, nothing can come close to the heartiness of this dish of goodness.

- 3 large russet potatoes, peeled and sliced 1/4-inch thick
- 1 large yellow onion, chopped
- 1/4 cup low-sodium vegetable broth
- 2 tablespoons low-sodium vegetable broth
- 1 teaspoon salt
  Pinch of black pepper
- 1 cup Plant to Plate Who Stole the Cheese? (pg. 89)
- 1/2 cup fresh dill, finely chopped

1. Preheat oven to 425 degrees.

2. In a 12-inch cast-iron skillet, sauté the onion in 1/4 cup of low-sodium vegetable broth until soft and golden, adding more liquid if needed. Do not burn. Once sautéed, spread onion in even layer in the skillet.

3. In a large bowl, add the potatoes, then add 2 tablespoons of low-sodium vegetable broth. Mix well to get the potatoes coated. Add salt, black pepper, and half of the Plant to Plate Who Stole the Cheese mixture, coating vegetables well.

4. Place the potato mixture in an even layer on top of the sautéed onion.

5. Cover the potatoes with the remaining Plant to Plate Who Stole the Cheese mixture, place in oven, and cook for 25 minutes or until potatoes are soft and golden.

6. Rest before serving.

7. Enjoy in the best of health!

Plant to Plate Orange Cranberry Loaf, pg. 121

Delightful Desserts

Who says eating plant-based has to be without a little dessert and sweetness in your life?

Take note of how much sugar you are consuming in a day. You may find yourself coming to the realization that you are addicted to sugar and want and need some kind of sugar fix in your day. I'll bet you've tried substituting with fake sugar. I promise you, sugar-free "food-like products" pale in comparison to the taste and healthiness in these desserts.

Go with as many natural plant-based foods as you need to satisfy your sweet tooth. Once you begin to taste fruit and all its sweetness, you will be on a path to better health.

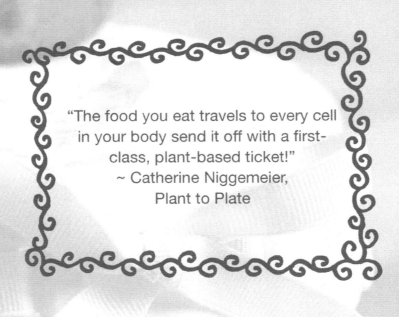

"The food you eat travels to every cell in your body send it off with a first-class, plant-based ticket!"
~ Catherine Niggemeier,
Plant to Plate

Plant to Plate
Citrus Bliss

MAKES 2 SERVINGS

I love this dish as a go-to breakfast, but it also works as the perfect dessert on a cold winter's night. Either way, it warms my heart and feeds my soul! Citrus is a big part of our morning routines in the Plant to Plate kitchen, and I truly believe it's why we stay healthy through our long, cold Long Island winters.

This dish makes your plate look joyful and alive. Do your best to add lots of color to your plate—your body, your eyes, and your mind will thank you. My favorite type of orange for this is Cara Cara!

- 1 **large ruby red grapefruit, peeled and segmented**
- 1 **large orange, peeled and segmented**
- 1/2 **cup walnuts**
- 1 **teaspoon agave**

1. Heat a large skillet on medium-high heat. Add the walnuts and toss continuously for 1–2 minutes until golden brown and you can smell the flavors being released. Remove from skillet and set aside.

2. In the same skillet, heat the grapefruit and oranges until seared, 2–3 minutes on each side. Do not overcook or you will dry out the citrus.

3. Plate the fruit, top with walnuts, and drizzle with agave or maple syrup.

4. Enjoy in the best of health!

Plant to Plate
Almond Orange Joy

MAKES ABOUT 24 PIECES

I prepared this recipe for a local news segment, and it created so much interest that my kitchen was flooded with calls asking about it! It's funny how a sweet treat will make people interested in better health.

- 2 **cups almonds**
- 1 **cup pitted dates**
   Juice and zest of 1 orange
- 1/8 **teaspoon salt**
- 1 **teaspoon vanilla**

1. In a food processor, blend all ingredients until the mixture comes together. Add more orange juice if needed to make the mixture stick together.

2. Scoop out and roll into 1-inch balls and place on a cookie sheet.

3. Chill in refrigerator for 1 hour, then serve.

4. Enjoy in the best of health!

> "There is no secret to good health. Eat your fruits and veggies!"
> ~ Catherine Niggemeier, Plant to Plate

Plant to Plate
Apple Nachos

MAKES 4 SERVINGS

When I first created this recipe for my girls, it was such a big hit, and they still love it today! You can add whatever you like to your apple nachos, so get creative. This is a great dessert to make with kids!

- 2 Gala apples, cored and thinly sliced
- 1/4 cup creamy organic natural peanut butter
- 2 tablespoons water
- 2 tablespoons shredded unsweetened coconut
- 1/4 cup raisins
- 1/4 cup mini chocolate chips

1. On a large platter, spread out your "nachos" (sliced apples) as your base layer.

2. Heat a small sauce pan on low to medium heat. Add peanut butter and 2 tablespoons of water. Stir until peanut butter becomes a sauce, slowly adding more water if needed.

3. Drizzle your "cheese" (peanut butter) over the apple slices and sprinkle with coconut, raisins, and chocolate chips.

4. Enjoy in the best of health!

Plant to Plate
Grilled Fruit Platter

MAKES 4–6 SERVINGS

This is a huge family favorite any time of year. Of course, the best time is summertime, when the fruits are at their sweetest, but nothing gets me through the New York winters more than grilled pineapple as a dessert. When others are running to the supermarket to bake during snowstorms, I load up the cart with pineapple. It's the best dessert I can give my taste buds and my heart!

Here are some of my favorite fruits to grill:

- 1 pineapple, cored and peeled
- 4 peaches, halved and pitted
- 12 large watermelon wedges

1. Slice the fruit.

2. Place on a heated grill and cook for 5 minutes on each side, or until you get the grill marks you desire.

3. Enjoy in the best of health!

> *"Don't panic if you didn't have plants at breakfast. Make up for it at lunch and dinner!"*
> *~ Catherine Niggemeier, Plant to Plate*

Plant to Plate Apple Nachos

"Every day you eat more plants,
you will thank yourself!"
~ Catherine Niggemeier,
Plant to Plate

Plant to Plate
Peanut Butter Balls

MAKES ABOUT 15 BALLS

Who doesn't love the heavenly combination of peanut butter and chocolate? If you don't, then I don't know what to say! This is the recipe that most often gets people to tell me that perhaps they can live plant-based after all!

- 1 cup organic natural creamy peanut butter
- 4 tablespoons pure maple or agave syrup
- 1/4 teaspoon fine sea salt
- 1/2 cup crispy rice cereal
- 3/4 cup dark chocolate chips
- 1/2 cup shredded unsweetened coconut

1. In a large bowl, mix together the peanut butter and maple syrup until it thickens up. If it's too dry, add a touch more syrup.

2. Add the salt, then stir in the cereal. Shape into small balls, about 1 inch in size.

3. In a small pot, add the chocolate chips and warm over low heat, stirring frequently. Once half the chips have melted, add in shredded coconut, remove from heat, and stir until smooth.

4. With a fork, dip the balls into the melted chocolate and place on platter. Chill balls in the refrigerator for 1 hour and serve.

5. Enjoy in the best of health!

Plant to Plate
Cookie Clusters

MAKES ABOUT 30 COOKIES

The trick to this recipe is very ripe bananas. The riper the banana, the sweeter the cookie. If you are a cookie-for-breakfast person, I say with this cookie, it is not a problem. I make big batches and store them in the freezer so we always have a sweet plant-based treat on hand.

- 3 ripe bananas
- 1/3 cup unsweetened applesauce
- 1 teaspoon vanilla
- 2 cups old-fashioned rolled oats
- 3 tablespoons cocoa powder
- 1/2 cup chopped walnuts
- 1/4 cup shredded unsweetened coconut
- 1/8 teaspoon salt

1. Preheat oven to 350 degrees.

2. In large bowl, mash the bananas with the tines of a fork, then add the applesauce and vanilla. Mix well.

3. Fold in the old-fashioned rolled oats, cocoa powder, walnuts, coconut, and salt.

4. Scoop out dough with a cookie scooper or a tablespoon and place on cookie sheet. Bake for 15 minutes per batch.

5. Enjoy in the best of health!

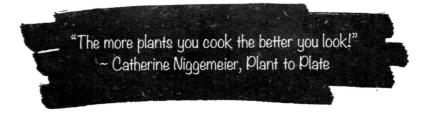

"The more plants you cook the better you look!"
~ Catherine Niggemeier, Plant to Plate

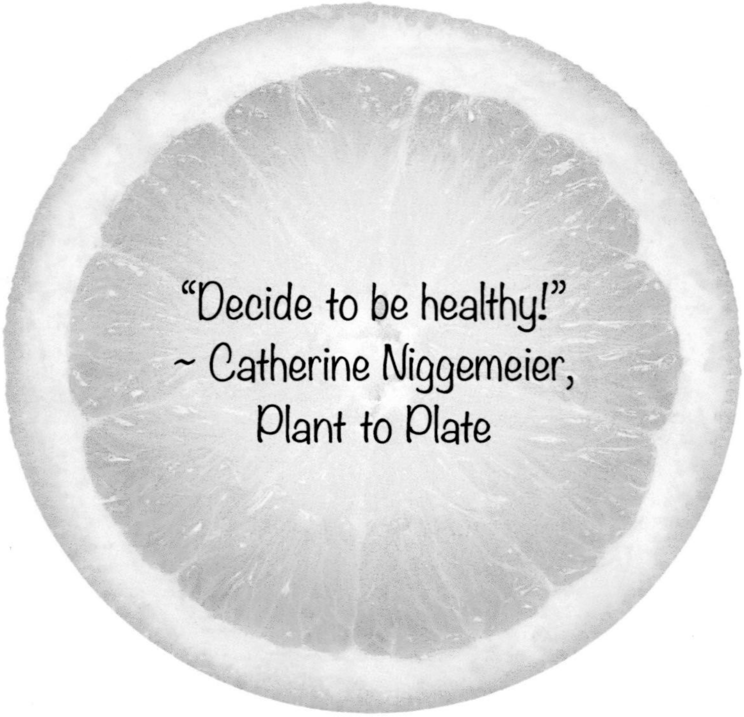

"Decide to be healthy!"
~ Catherine Niggemeier,
Plant to Plate

Plant to Plate Orange Cranberry Loaf

MAKES 1 LOAF

I don't think anyone wants to live their life without a little cake, so here is my recipe for a delicious plant-based dessert. Full disclaimer: I live each day eating a whole-food, plant-based diet, so I rarely eat processed foods, but in this case, I use vegan/plant-based butter and sugar.

2	cups all-purpose flour
1/2	teaspoon baking powder
1/2	teaspoon baking soda
1/2	teaspoon salt
	Zest of 1 orange
1-1/2	cups fresh cranberries
1/2	cup chopped pecans
1/4	cup plant-based butter
1/2	cup sugar
3/4	cup orange juice
	Plant-based egg substitute (pg. 35)

1. Preheat oven to 350 degrees. Spray a 9 × 5 loaf pan with nonstick cooking spray.

2. In a large bowl, mix the flour, baking powder, baking soda, salt, orange zest, cranberries, and pecans.

3. In a separate bowl, combine the plant-based butter, sugar, plant-based egg substitute, and orange juice. Mix well and add to dry ingredients.

4. Pour mixture into pan and bake for 1 hour.

5. Remove from oven and let cool for 30 minutes.

6. Enjoy in the best of health!

Resources

If you're looking to fully embrace a whole-food, plant-based lifestyle, here are some excellent resources to guide you on your journey to better health. The more you connect with resources like these in your daily life, the better your chances are for adopting a whole-food, plant-based lifestyle. All of these organizations offer a great sense of community and support, and I am proud to be associated with many of them. I encourage you to sign up for their newsletters and connect on social media.

T. Colin Campbell Center for Nutrition Studies
nutritionstudies.org

PlantPureNation.com

PlantPureCommunities.org

Physicians Committee for Responsible Medicine www.pcrm.org

Films

Forks Over Knives available at
www.forksoverknives.com
Netflix, iTunes or Amazon

PlantPure Nation available at
www.PlantPureNation.com
Netflix, iTunes or Amazon

Eating You Alive available at
www.eatingyoualive.com

Books

The China Study: The Most Comprehensive Study of Nutrition Ever Conducted And the Startling Implications for Diet, Weight Loss, And Long-term Health by Thomas Campbell and T. Colin Campbell

Whole: Rethinking the Science of Nutrition by T. Colin Campbell and Howard Jacobson

The China Study Cookbook: Over 120 Whole Food, Plant-Based Recipes by LeAnne Campbell and Steven Campbell Disla

The PlantPure Nation Cookbook: The Official Companion Cookbook to the Breakthrough Film...with over 150 Plant-Based Recipes by Kim Campbell and T. Colin Campbell

The PlantPure Kitchen: 130 Mouthwatering, Whole Food Recipes and Tips for a Plant-Based Life by Kim Campbell and T. Colin Campbell

The Forks Over Knives Plan: How to Transition to the Life-Saving, Whole-Food, Plant-Based Diet by Alona Pulde M.D. and Matthew Lederman, M.D.

Dr. Neal Barnard's Program for Reversing Diabetes: The Scientifically Proven System for Reversing Diabetes without Drugs by Neal Barnard, M.D.

The Cheese Trap: How Breaking a Surprising Addiction Will Help You Lose Weight, Gain Energy, and Get Healthy by Neal Barnard, M.D.

Acknowledgments

To those who helped me transform my health and Plant to Plate for the better.

To Dr. Campbell and "The China Study," this is where it all began, and I am forever grateful for your science and insight, which changed my health for the better. Dr. Campbell, your mission to help others through your non-profit nutrition organization is a continuous gift to me and so many.

To Nelson and Kim Campbell, your endless work through PlantPure Nation to build stronger, healthier, and more sustainable communities through research and policy continues to change the lives of many for the better each and every day, and I am honored to know both of you.

To Patty Corry, your phone call in March of 2015 asking me to be an ambassador for the film, *Plant-Pure Nation*, changed so much for me and opened so many doors, and I am better for knowing you. Your beauty shines from the inside out!

To John Corry, *PlantPure Nation* and *Forks Over Knives* are compelling stories that continue to inspire me to help people make healthier decisions for their overall health, and I am grateful for the work you do. It was an honor to have you and your amazing production team in the Plant to Plate Kitchen, and it was certainly one of the best plant-based days of my life!

To the T. Colin Campbell Center for Nutrition Studies, your certificate in plant-based nutrition enriched my education and confidence in sharing the important message of what a whole-food, plant-based lifestyle can do for one's health. I am a proud graduate, and I continue to share your endeavors with clients to change their health for the better through a whole-food, plant-based lifestyle.

To all my clients, who continue to support and share their enthusiasm for this girl, who you really took a chance on by attending dinners in the Plant to Plate Kitchen. I am forever grateful and wish you a life filled with plants and love!

To my editor, Crystal Watanabe of Pikko's House, your guidance and encouragement has carried me through, and it would not have been possible without you by my side, holding my hand from 5,000 miles away. Thank you for all of your help!

To Dori Smith, your friendship, laughter, and weekly words of encouragement mean the world to me, and you are the best cheerleader a girl could have.

To Timothy Butler Photography, thank you for capturing the essence of my food and for being so great to work with.

To Deborah at Tugboat Design, thank you for bringing my book to life and for guiding me through the publishing process.

To Physicians Committee for Responsible Medicine, thank you for accepting me into your Food for Life Program. I am proud to be an instructor of your amazing, life-changing message of health.

To Mary Mucci of *News12 Long Island*, thank you for joining me in the Plant to Plate Kitchen and for allowing me to share my message of health through your amazing program, *Long Island Naturally*. Your program is so needed and continues to shed light on the importance of health and wellness to so many.

To Cornucopia Sayville, New York, your food carried me through in the beginning of my health journey and gave me the inspiration to create beautiful plant-based dishes of my own. Thank you for your continued support and your endless supply of amazing plants.

KeithFrawley.com, thank you for your creative designs! The website and logo you created brought Plant to Plate Education to a whole new level. You are amazing to work with and your knowledge is endless.

To Bruno Mars, Barry White, Madonna, Diana Ross, Beyoncé, Gwen Stefani, Pink, Katy Perry, ABBA, Justin Timberlake, Meghan Trainor, Stevie Wonder, Ed Sheeran, Adele, and many more, thanks for making my daily exercise all the more fun and enjoyable!

And finally, to Darby Duchess, the best walking companion and fur baby a family could love.

"Mother Earth planted the garden.
Make sure you eat from it!"
~ Catherine Niggemeier, Plant to Plate

About the Author

Catherine McMenamin Niggemeier is the founder of Plant to Plate Education Corporation, a certified business offering education and inspiration in plant-based nutrition. In 2014, at the age of forty-six, Catherine switched to a whole-food, plant-based lifestyle and lost eighty pounds in less than a year.

After obtaining a certificate from the T. Colin Campbell Center for Nutrition Studies at Cornell University, Catherine started her first cooking class with five people and eventually built Plant to Plate into a thriving business, teaching more than 1,000 clients how to eat whole-food, plant-based. With the support of her husband, Steve, Catherine expanded her business and education. She is also a certified instructor through the Physicians Committee for Responsible Medicine's *Food for Life* program. Catherine is an ambassador for the documentary *PlantPure Nation* and works diligently to promote this important film so that others can hear the message of one of the most important health breakthroughs of all time. She has a love of learning and focuses her business on bringing the best information to improve the health of her clients.

She is a certified health and wellness coach through the Institute for Integrative Nutrition and has expanded her business from teaching to include public speaking and employee-wellness programs. She has been featured on television, appearing on *News 12 Long Island* and *Newsday*.

When Catherine isn't sharing her message of health with others, she enjoys traveling and spending time at the beach, playing tennis, or anything outdoors with Steve and their two plant-loving daughters, Hannah and Ava. She also shares her love with her constant walking companion, her golden retriever, Darby. She lives in the beautiful town of Sayville, New York, where she has felt the love and support from many people in her community. She is thankful that life took this turn and is excited about having a positive influence on the future health of others.

She continues to create new recipes and share her message of health with others online. You can reach her at her website www.planttoplateeducation.com and follow her on the following social media channels:

Facebook: facebook.com/
Plant-to-Plate-Education-424314537734686/
Instagram: @planttoplateeducation
Twitter: @planttoplateed
LinkedIn: Catherine McMenamin Niggemeier

Alphabetical Recipe Index

Made in the USA
Coppell, TX
12 February 2021